S0-BYP-913

*THROUGH
THE BIBLE
WITH THOSE
WHO WERE THERE*

*Through*

G. Allen Fleece Library
Columbia International University
Columbia, SC 29203

# the Bible
## with those
### who were there

A Guide to the Scriptures
by Harold and Carole
Straughn

TYNDALE HOUSE Publishers, Inc.
*Wheaton, Illinois*
Coverdale House Publishers Ltd.
*London, England*

C. Allen Fleece Library
Columbia International University
Columbia, SC 29203

Library of Congress
Catalog Card Number
74-19646
ISBN 8423-7150-8
Copyright © 1975
Tyndale House Publishers, Inc.,
Wheaton, Illinois.
All rights reserved.
First printing, January 1975
Printed in the
United States of America

# CONTENTS

How to Get Started

# HOW TO GET STARTED

This guided tour through the Bible, you'll quickly discover, is different. It's more like an expedition than a course of study. That's because a course that takes you through the world of the Bible ranges across many centuries and three continents. You'll be swept into a different world and age. When you land at your first destination, Mesopotamia, you will meet the wealthy tent-dwelling patriarch Abraham, and you will accompany him through the dusty and rugged world he lived in. You will hear about his ancestors, all the way back to Adam and Eve, Cain and Abel, Noah and his sons. You will meet Abraham's family: his wife Sarah; his son Isaac; his grandson, the opportunistic Jacob; Jacob's twelve bickering sons. Then you will be taken closer to home (but not much), settling down in Egypt in the second millennium B.C. You will leave twelve sons of Jacob and follow their descendants into 400 years of slavery, and then, being led by Moses, escape to freedom, only to wander for forty years in the Sinai Desert. And so it goes for the next thousand years or so before the time of Christ.

We've planned for you to get well acquainted with a few of the great personalities: David and Jeremiah, Jesus, Peter and Paul. If you were to meet too many people, their names

would become a blur. Even so, there is plenty of
atmosphere: the empires of Babylon, Greece and Rome;
little known, ordinary people who met Jesus and registered
their impressions of him; a passing scene of warriors,
tentmakers, fishermen, prophets, angels.

We've tried very hard to arrange this tour so that it
avoids falling into propaganda for a particular viewpoint.
When we finish we want to leave you free to decide whether
you want to see more. You may already be convinced of the
value of the biblical venture. We hope this tour will
reinforce your expectations. On the other hand, if you
have only a nodding acquaintance with those people, you
might decide that the way is too demanding, too full of
surprises and risks. Even if you consider yourself neutral, or
an agnostic, this guide through the Bible can give you a
clear view of what it is you've decided against.

A lot of people today enjoy the fruit, but neglect the root,
of the biblical way—they enjoy love and peace, they believe
in justice and freedom, without knowing much about how it
all began. If the roots are neglected long enough, the fruit
will eventually disappear.

*Planning Your Schedule*
This tour is intended to take you about eight weeks. But you
can go as fast or as slowly as you wish. You can proceed all
by yourself, or with your family, or in a group. The
itinerary is divided into eight parts, each part taking you a
little over an hour. Each part is divided into six sections that
take ten to fifteen minutes each. So if you want to, you can
carve out your time by the hour (an easy way to find that
much time is to pass up some TV programs you don't care
much about). Or you can do it in 15-minute slices—when
you wake up, before you go to bed, during a coffee break,
waiting for an appointment, as part of your afternoon siesta.

You can travel light. This guide book is all you need: the
biblical references we discuss are included.

*The Tour Begins*
The procedure couldn't be simpler. Just start with Part One.
After a short time you'll come to some stopping places
where you can look back and try to absorb what you've
experienced. We do this with two check-lists. One is called

# XI HOW TO GET STARTED

"Getting the Story in Mind." It helps you to remember the most important things that happen. The other is called "Getting the Meaning in Hand." It gives you a chance to use your ingenuity in making practical use of what you've found.

To help you Get the Story in Mind, we often take you back to the Bible where you can look it up for yourself. To help you Get the Meaning in Hand, we point out areas of modern life where you can explore the meaning it has for you today.

As a bonus, you'll be offered Side Trips every so often. Follow them up if they appeal to you; they're optional.

One last thing. There's the language problem. Most of the Old Testament peoples spoke Hebrew or Aramaic, with some Akkadian and Ugaritic thrown in. Most of the New Testament figures spoke Aramaic (Hebrew), Latin, or Greek. What if it's *all* Greek to you? Fortunately, every word of the Bible has been translated into English for 500 years. In fact, the problem is to decide which English translation to use. In just a few years, *The Living Bible* has proved one of the most popular translations of all. We like its clear, vivid wording and its ability to cross time and space barriers, without compromising accuracy or relevance. As your "companion" to *The Living Bible*, we hope through this course to accompany you and to share with you the spiritual adventure that a journey through the Word of God has offered to every generation.

If you have another translation at home, you may want to use it as well. Comparison is the simplest form of commentary. If you're thinking of buying a Bible, we suggest one of the newer translations such as *The Living Bible*. Ask a bookstore dealer to show you several. Look up your favorite passages and see how they speak to you.

The advantages of a modern language version notwithstanding, the 350-year-old King James Version still is the favorite of millions. Its majestic Elizabethan language, though at times difficult to understand, will remain a classic of English literature.

Speaking of King James, may we borrow a phrase from his time to wish you well: *God bee w' ye,* people used to say as they parted company. Today we just abbreviate it and say,

*Good-bye.*

# Part One

# ABRAHAM

## A Man Believes God and Is Rewarded

# 1 Beginning in the Book of Beginnings / *Genesis 1–11*

Abraham is a hero for three faiths, the Jewish, the Muslim, and the Christian. The Jewish and Arab peoples look to him as their national ancestor. Christians see him as their spiritual ancestor, and call him "the father of the faithful." Each of the groups sees itself as part of the fulfillment of promises God made to Abraham, promises which thread throughout the Bible.

One end of the thread begins in *Genesis*, the first book of the Old Testament and of the Bible. The word genesis means "beginnings." The first eleven chapters of this book lead up to Abraham. The next fifteen chapters are about Abraham himself. The rest of the book of *Genesis* tells how the promises to Abraham work out in the life of his son Isaac, his grandson Jacob, and his great-grandson Joseph. Actually, the rest of the Bible is the story of what happens to his descendants as they grow from a tribe into a nation, and from a nation into a universal community, the church.

Why was it necessary for God to call one man from

among the thousands of his contemporaries? And why one
people from among the many nations around them? The first
eleven chapters of *Genesis* answer this question. These few
pages give us the background of mankind up to the call of
Abraham.

We read first how the world of nature we see around
us—heaven and earth, land and sea, green vegetation, living
animals, and the rolling seasons—all are the good creation of a
trustworthy God. The last and best of the creation was
mankind, male and female. These the creator set among
and over his other creatures.

Man (in the Hebrew language *Adam*) was created out of the
dust of the ground (in Hebrew *adamah*). Even so, he was the
one creature made in God's own image. His task was to
cultivate his garden home and to rule the other creatures.
God created man to offer trusting obedience of his own free
will. In doing so God took a risk. It would also be possible for
man to use his freedom to turn against God. Man's trust in
God was tested by the presence of a forbidden tree in the
middle of the garden.

Adam and his wife Eve disobeyed God, because they
doubted that he really had their best interest at heart. They
hoped that the forbidden fruit would bring them God-like
power. Instead, it brought them a host of troubles. Thorns
infested the once-fruitful earth. Adam had to toil for his
living instead of just gathering his food from the trees.
Where once mankind could have had only peace and joy and
friendship with God, now they were doomed to pain, disease,
and unending labor until their brief life flickered out and
their bodies turned back into the dust of the earth from
which they came.

After the first sin, men went from bad to worse. Adam's
son Cain killed his brother Abel. Technical advance brought
only further moral decay until mankind was almost totally
corrupt, capable of doing and even of thinking only evil
continually. To all human appearances God's whole
experiment in freedom for mankind was a colossal failure.
The human race seemed bent on destruction.

But God found one faithful man, Noah, and through him
planned to save mankind and the other species from
extinction. God told Noah to build a huge houseboat, or

ark, in which Noah's own family and pairs of all the air-breathing animals and birds were saved. Following the disastrous flood, these creatures came out of the ark to begin life on earth again.

After this fresh start, however, men soon reverted to their old ways. The unfinished tower of Babel stood as a monument to their misplaced pride in their own self-sufficiency. Because they tried to build a tower to heaven, men became scattered throughout the world into feuding nations of thousands of "babbling" tongues, suffering a communications barrier that has continued to plague the world.

The resulting disharmony among men and between men and God could not be cured by man himself. It was to take an act of God—or rather the continuing act of God—to save man from his own destruction. The call of Abraham is that divine act which starts in motion God's great plan of salvation.

## Getting the Story in Mind

On the left are some of the "beginnings" described in Genesis, the Book of Beginnings. On the right are some of the people connected with these beginnings. Match people with events by writing the correct letter by each number.

_____ 1. *The first people*            *a. Cain and Abel*
_____ 2. *The first murder*           *b. Abraham*
_____ 3. *The first natural disaster*  *c. Adam and Eve*
_____ 4. *The first communications*    *d. Babel Tower builders*
       *gap*                               *e. Noah*
_____ 5. *The first promise of a*
       *great nation*

## Getting the Meaning in Hand

In each sentence, check the phrase that best describes the teachings of the opening chapters of Genesis.

1 *The opening chapters of the Book of Genesis are basically*
_____ *a. scientific research on the origins of the species.*
_____ *b. primitive mythology of value now only to children.*

_____ c. *religious teachings about the relation of God and man in the world.*

_____ d. *ancient history of interest to experts.*

2 *Man is free to do*

_____ a. *anything he puts his mind to.*

_____ b. *only what God has planned for him.*

_____ c. *what is harmful to him as well as what is good.*

_____ d. *only what is best for him.*

3 *The world of nature is pictured as*

_____ a. *a brutal scene of violent struggle.*

_____ b. *a paradise of endless natural resources for man to enjoy.*

_____ c. *a world that man is to subdue and to care for.*

_____ d. *a place to which the human race is confined.*

4 *When it comes to choosing a place to live,*

_____ a. *the city is best because of its cultural and employment opportunities.*

_____ b. *the countryside is best because of its peace and quiet.*

_____ c. *man is capable of both good and evil no matter where he lives.*

_____ d. *the world is really a terrible place to live.*

5 *When men first began to build tall buildings,*

_____ a. *they thought uppermost about protection and comfort.*

_____ b. *they were trying to become god-like.*

_____ c. *they were able to bring the people closer together.*

_____ d. *they wanted to show their dependence on God.*

6 *As man becomes more civilized*

_____ a. *he gradually becomes more moral than the ancient primitive tribes.*

_____ b. *his power for progress and for destruction is multiplied.*

_____ c. *he loses his need for religion.*

_____ d. *he would be better off to return to the simple life of the ancient world.*

# 2 A Good Man Takes a Risk / *Genesis 12*

The good God shaped a good creation and crowned it with mankind made in God's own image. Loving, trusting obedience offered to God of man's own free will was worth the risk that he might also turn against God. And turn against God man did. Life without God was much more attractive for the vast majority. A man could do what comes naturally. He could look out for Number One. He could take the course of least resistance. But here and there somebody would choose to serve the Creator instead of the creatures.

In Ur, in Mesopotamia, the land of the arrogant Babel Tower builders, God found another faithful man, Abram, or Abraham as he was later called. His father had taken him from Ur to Harran, the capital city of the people who prevailed in Mesopotamia in those days.

(Book of Genesis Chapter 12 verses 1 through 3) *After the death of Abram's father, God told him, "Leave your own country behind you, and your own people, and go to the land I will guide you to. If you do, I will cause you to become the father of a great nation; I will bless you and make your name famous, and you will be a blessing to many others. I will bless those who bless you and curse those who curse you; and the entire world will be blessed because of you."*

In deciding how to answer the call of God, Abraham had hardly anything to go on but God's word. What would he have to gain by leaving his home country, his relatives and his friends, by uprooting his wife, his family, and his other dependents from their familiar surroundings? The direction God was pointing was into the southern desert, so the promised land did not then look very promising.

But Abraham trusted God's promise; he believed that Jehovah, his God, would be with him wherever he went. His God was not bound to a particular rock, tree, or country, but was the maker of heaven and earth. God had promised to give him many descendants. That was a prize he longed for, because even though he was wealthy, he still had no heirs. Abraham decided the prize was greater than the risk, even though he and his wife were very old.

**Genesis 12:4, 5** *So Abram departed as the Lord had instructed him, and Lot went too; Abram was seventy-five years old at that time. He took his wife Sarai, his nephew Lot, and all his wealth—the cattle and slaves he had gotten in Haran—and finally arrived in Canaan.*

After they arrived in the promised land, they had to face many difficulties. There were wars and famines. They always felt themselves foreigners in this land that was supposed to be theirs. Although the Lord blessed Abraham with wealth and protected him and Sarai from danger, they had to wait twenty-five years for the son God had promised. It was enough to try the faith of any person. Because Abraham passed the test, he will always be known and loved as the "father of the faithful."

## Getting the Story in Mind

Are you lost? Here is a map to guide you:

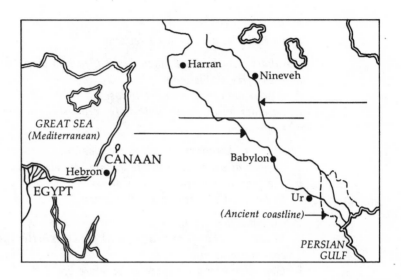

1 *"Mesopotamia" is a word meaning "land between the rivers."*
*Write it in the blank provided on the map.*

2 *The two great rivers of Mesopotamia are known as the Tigris (top)*
*and the Euphrates (bottom). Write the names of these two rivers*
*in the right blanks on the map.*

3 *Draw a line to follow Abraham's journeys. Beginning at Ur, pass*
*through Harran, to the land of Canaan; then to Egypt, and back*
*to Hebron.*

4 *With his flocks and herds Abraham passed through the rich and*
*well-watered land we call the Fertile Crescent, often believed to*
*be the "cradle of civilization." With your pencil, shade in the*
*area of the map on either side of Abraham's route to indicate the*
*Fertile Crescent. (Begin at Persian Gulf; end in Egypt.)*

## Getting the Meaning in Hand

Make a check mark by the phrase that best completes the
sentence.

1 *When Abraham obeyed God and left his country,*
_____ *a. he thought it over for a long time.*

_____ *b. he took a risk on faith.*
_____ *c. he took the path of least resistance.*

2 *Abraham's style of life when God called him was that of*
_____ *a. a carefree single man.*
_____ *b. a poor man with nothing to lose.*
_____ *c. an older businessman with wife, property, and many*
        *responsibilities.*

3 *The reason Abraham left his home was:*
_____ *a. he was dissatisfied with life among his relatives.*
_____ *b. the grass looked greener in Canaan.*
_____ *c. he believed in a trustworthy promise.*

4 *When Abraham got to Canaan*
_____ *a. he found that a life of struggle with God was better than a life of*
        *ease without him.*
_____ *b. God gave him a prosperous, carefree life.*
_____ *c. life with God was a letdown.*

## Side Trip

Here's something to think about as you have time: "I will
curse those who curse you." What does it mean for God to
curse someone? Does that contradict the compassion of
God? Would you like for God to be on your side and to
punish those who curse you? You may want to read and
write about this subject. Most libraries have commentaries on
the Book of Genesis; so do many churches: consult some to
see how they treat Genesis 12:1-4. Most Bible dictionaries
and concordances contain helpful information under
"Blessing" and "Curse." They are the basic tools for your
own independent Bible study.

## 3 Abraham Shows Compassion and Is Rewarded / Genesis 18:1-14

God spoke to Abraham many times and in many ways, sometimes by visions, by dreams, or by angels. But things were different when he came to announce the birth of the son, who would be the beginning of a great nation. When the Lord appeared to Abraham by the terebinth trees of Mamre, Abraham did not even recognize him at first.

Genesis 18:1-5
*One hot summer afternoon as he was sitting in the opening of his tent, he suddenly noticed three men coming toward him. He sprang up and ran to meet them and welcomed them.*

*"Sirs," he said, "please don't go any further. Stop awhile and rest here in the shade of this tree while I get water to refresh your feet, and a bite to eat to strengthen you. Do stay awhile before continuing your journey."*

*"All right," they said, "do as you have said."*

Abraham spared no effort to serve his unknown guests. First, he hurried to Sarah in the tent and urged her to bake some fresh cakes as quickly as possible.

# 10 ABRAHAM: A MAN BELIEVES GOD AND IS REWARDED

Genesis
18:7, 8 *Then he ran out to the herd and selected a fat calf and told a servant to hurry and butcher it. Soon, taking them cheese and milk and the roast veal, he set it before the men and stood beneath the trees beside them as they ate.*

Although Abraham was a great chieftain, he did not leave it to his servants to bake the bread, he had his own wife to do it, and he did not have a servant bring their food, but waited on them himself.

All this he did while unaware that he was serving the Lord God himself and two of his angels who had taken human form.

After the three men had enjoyed the fine roasted veal, the fresh cakes, and cottage cheese that Abraham served them, they began to reveal the real purpose of their coming.

Genesis
18:9, 10 *"Where is Sarah, your wife?" they asked him.*
*"In the tent," Abraham replied.*
*Then the Lord said, "Next year I will give you and Sarah a son!"*

In those days it was not the custom for the women to eat with the men. But that did not keep Sarah from following the conversation with great interest from behind the thin tent wall. She pricked up her ears when she heard her name mentioned and was astounded to hear this prediction, which, according to all the rules of common sense could not possibly come true.

Genesis
18:11, 12 *Now Abraham and Sarah were both very old, and Sarah was long since past the time when she could have a baby.*
*So Sarah laughed silently. "A woman my age have a baby?" she scoffed to herself. "And with a husband as old as mine?"*

But Sarah had another surprise waiting for her. The stranger who had spoken had also heard her silent reply to his words.

Genesis
18:13, 14 *"Why did Sarah laugh? Why did she say 'Can an old woman like me have a baby?' Is anything too hard for God? Next year, just as I told you, I will certainly see to it that Sarah has a son."*

Frightened by having her secret thoughts suddenly

revealed, Sarah tried to deny that she had laughed, but the Lord said, "Yes, you did laugh."

When the promised son was at last born to Sarah then she laughed for joy. Abraham named the boy Isaac, which means "laughter" and Sarah said:

Genesis
21:6, 7

*"God has brought me laughter! All who hear about this shall rejoice with me. For who would have dreamed that I would ever have a baby? Yet I have given Abraham a child in his old age!"*

Long afterwards this story was told by Abraham's descendants as an example of how God expects his followers to treat people who are different from themselves. They themselves were once foreigners in a land not their own. Well was the memory preserved as father taught son throughout countless generations what it was like to have no land of their own. The story of Abraham's courtesy to the three strangers that hot afternoon was used to show the value of compassionate action for people who are in need.

## Getting the Story in Mind

Check the best ending for each sentence:

1 *When Abraham saw three strangers approaching his camp,*
_____ *a. he treated them as honored guests.*
_____ *b. he gave them the leftovers from his noon meal.*
_____ *c. he warned them to go away and leave him alone.*

2 *In deciding how to treat the strangers Abraham*
_____ *a. worried about robbers who might be nearby.*
_____ *b. worried about his food budget.*
_____ *c. worried about how tired and hungry the men might be.*

3 *When Sarah overheard the strangers saying she would have a baby, she*
_____ *a. believed.*
_____ *b. wept.*
_____ *c. laughed.*

4 *The story of Abraham and the three visitors was told by his descendants*
_____ *a. to show that God often appeared in human form.*
_____ *b. to show that God seldom appeared in human form.*

_____ c. *as an example of compassionate action for people who are in
need.*
_____ d. *to show that the messengers were fanatics or imposters.*

## Getting the Meaning in Hand

Compassion for someone you do not know costs something.
You take a risk to be kind to someone of a different
background or class or race. To do it you must have faith
that God will reward you as he rewarded Abraham.

Here is a list of "strangers" we often encounter today.
Which ones fit most directly your own situation? (Check at
least three.)

_____ 1. *new family in the neighborhood*
_____ 2. *person of another social class, religion, or race*
_____ 3. *children who play near your home*
_____ 4. *a shy or new person at the office*
_____ 5. *the "invisible" strangers in rest homes, mental hospitals*
_____ 6. *strangers in other parts of the world*
_____ 7. *strangers who consider themselves your enemy*
_____ 8. *strangers on the other side of the generation gap*
_____ 9. *strangers in your own family*

# 4 Abraham Negotiates with God / *Genesis 18:16-33*

When the three strangers stopped at Abraham's tent, they had not only a birth announcement to give, but a death warrant also. The injustice and callous living of the great majority had reached fever pitch again, increasing ever since the time of the great flood.

In comparison to a just and holy God, the people in the city of Sodom fell particularly short. The wild orgies and excesses of all kinds that took place in that city have helped its name to be a permanent symbol of decadence. Were these people headed for destruction and the wrath of God?

Because of Abraham's relationship to him, God decided to discuss the matter with him. Abraham had a special interest in the city of Sodom because it was the home of his nephew, Lot, who had come with him out of Harran.

The following story unfolds a fascinating discussion about the fate of an infamous city between God and a man who truly could be called the friend of God.

# 14 ABRAHAM: A MAN BELIEVES GOD AND IS REWARDED

Genesis
18:17-33

*"Should I hide my plan from Abraham?" God asked. "For Abraham shall become a mighty nation, and he will be a source of blessing for all the nations of the earth. And I have picked him out to have godly descendants and a godly household—men who are just and good—so that I can do for him all I have promised."*

*So the Lord told Abraham, "I have heard that the people of Sodom and Gomorrah are utterly evil, and that everything they do is wicked. I am going down to see whether these reports are true or not. Then I will know." So the other two went on toward Sodom, but the Lord remained with Abraham a while. Then Abraham approached him and said, "Will you kill good and bad alike? Suppose you find fifty godly people there within the city—will you destroy it, and not spare it for their sakes? That wouldn't be right! Surely you wouldn't do such a thing, to kill the godly with the wicked! Why, you would be treating godly and wicked exactly the same! Surely you wouldn't do that! Should not the Judge of all the earth be fair?"*

*And God replied, "If I find fifty godly people there, I will spare the entire city for their sake."*

*Then Abraham spoke again. "Since I have begun, let me go on and speak further to the Lord, though I am but dust and ashes. Suppose there are only forty-five? Will you destroy the city for lack of five?"*

*And God said, "I will not destroy it if I find forty-five."*

*Then Abraham went further with his request. "Suppose there are only forty?"*

*And God replied, "I won't destroy it if there are forty."*

*"Please don't be angry," Abraham pleaded. "Let me speak: suppose only thirty are found there?"*

*And God replied, "I won't do it if there are thirty there."*

*Then Abraham said, "Since I have dared to speak to God, let me continue—Suppose there are only twenty?"*

*And God said, "Then I won't destroy it for the sake of the twenty."*

*Finally, Abraham said, "Oh, let not the Lord be angry; I will speak but this once more! Suppose only ten are found?"*

*And God said, "Then, for the sake of the ten, I won't destroy it."*

*And the Lord went on his way when he had finished his conversation with Abraham. And Abraham returned to his tent.*

As you might have guessed, Abraham's bargaining in this case was in vain, for God was unable to find more than four righteous persons at the most—and even they were hardly the moral giants we might wish to look to as models.

The case of the Sodomites is exactly opposite from that of Abraham. When the angels, disguised as men, came to Lot's house, hospitality gave way to horror.

Genesis 19:4, 5 *After the meal, as they were preparing to retire for the night, the men of the city—yes, Sodomites, young and old from all over the city—surrounded the house and shouted to Lot, "Bring out those men to us so we can rape them."*

At great risk to himself and his family, Lot refused to do this. The angels protected him as he had tried to protect them. Then, because Lot alone had shown them kindness, it was Lot alone, with his family, who was saved when the city was destroyed.

## Getting the Story in Mind

From your reading and the above story about Abraham's negotiation with God over the fate of the city of Sodom, mark the following statements *True* or *False*.

_____ 1. *The Lord considered Abraham, a mere man, too insignificant a person to discuss his plans with.*

_____ 2. *The Lord wished to tell Abraham his plans concerning Sodom and Gomorrah as part of his lifelong care and nurture of him.*

_____ 3. *As the men turned to leave Abraham and continue on down to Sodom, Abraham came near the Lord, wishing to continue the conversation.*

_____ 4. *Abraham asked God if he intended to destroy good people along with the wicked.*

_____ 5. *The Lord was appearing to Abraham in the form of a man.*

_____ 6. *God did not listen to Abraham's side of the case.*

_____ 7. *God did not stop answering Abraham's pleas until Abraham himself stopped making them.*

_____ 8. *God would have saved everyone in Sodom if ten good people could be found.*

_____ 9. *Not even ten good people could be found.*

_____ 10. *The citizens of Sodom treated the strangers with respect and hospitality.*

# 5 Abraham's Greatest Test / *Genesis 22*

After Isaac was born, Abraham concentrated on rearing his son to carry on the faith so that Isaac's children and grandchildren might inherit God's promises.

Abraham and Isaac must have worshiped God many times together by offering fine young beasts, the best of the young cattle, sheep, or goats, to God upon the handmade altar of stone. Perhaps the ritual seems barbaric to us. The young animal's throat was slit, its blood flowing out upon the ground, a symbol of the life the worshiper had received from God. The life of the animal was poured out as a substitute for the life of the worshiper, whose guilt for sin made him worthy of death in God's righteous eyes. Then a fire was lit and the animal was either cooked and eaten or burned to ashes.

Isaac was receiving the training in faith from his father, that even though life can be hard and cruel, no matter how hard things seem, to trust God and to follow his will for your life is the most important thing there is, and worth far more than the price. Being God's friend is then worth the sacrifice of anything else.

Anything else? Could Abraham give up his son—his only son—for God? God wished to find out. The test he gave Abraham was also a test for Isaac's faith. Was Abraham's effort to pass on his faith taking root in his son?

Genesis 22:1, 2

*"Abraham!" God called.*

*"Yes, Lord?" he replied.*

*"Take with you your only son—yes, Isaac whom you love so much—and go to the land of Moriah and sacrifice him there as a burnt offering upon one of the mountains which I'll point out to you!"*

Abraham's thoughts at this chilling command are unknown to us. All we are told is:

Genesis 22:3

*The next morning Abraham got up early, chopped wood for a fire upon the altar, saddled his donkey, and took with him his son Isaac and two young men who were his servants, and started off to the place where God had told him to go.*

We are reminded of the first response Abraham had made to God's call back in Ur of the Chaldees. Not knowing just where he is going, but depending upon God's guidance, he follows without flinching. He gets up early in the morning. He seems to do most of the preparation himself—now as an old man, he chops the firewood himself, and he sets out once again. The first time he had set out with only the promise of a multitude of descendants, and no child at all. Now he sets out again, expecting to lose the child of promise.

Genesis 22:4, 5

*On the third day of the journey Abraham saw the place in the distance.*

*"Stay here with the donkey," Abraham told the young men, "and the lad and I will travel yonder and worship, and then come right back."*

"The lad and I ... will come right back." Did Abraham believe those words? How he must have grieved as he thought of

the part Isaac must play in the worship! Grimly he placed
the firewood on the boy's own shoulders, while he himself
carried the fire and the knife. To Isaac, who knew well the
ritual, the prepararations seemed incomplete:

Genesis     *Abraham placed the wood for the burnt offering upon Isaac's*
22:6-8 *shoulders, while he himself carried the knife and the flint for*
*striking a fire. So the two of them went on together.*
*"Father," Isaac asked, "we have the wood and the flint to*
*make the fire, but where is the lamb for the sacrifice?"*
*"God will see to it, my son," Abraham replied. And they went*
*on.*

Isaac shared his father's trust that God would provide the
sacrifice. He also fully trusted his father, but how that trust
was tested as preparations for the sacrifice continued!

Genesis     *When they arrived at the place where God had told Abraham to*
22:9 *go, he built an altar and placed the wood in order, ready for the*
*fire, and then tied Isaac and laid him on the altar over the wood.*

As it began to dawn upon Isaac who that young beast for the
sacrifice was to be, did he think of running away? Could he
have run away? We hear of no struggle. Did trust conquer
fear? Both father and son must have wondered how God
could possibly be the good God who had been their friend
for so long; still they resigned themselves to the mystery of
his will. They continued to trust and to follow his word.

Genesis *And Abraham took the knife and lifted it up to plunge it into his*
22:10 *son, to slay him.*

## Getting the Story in Mind

Mark these questions *True* or *False*, based on the story you
have just read.

_____  1. *Abraham wasn't sure whether it was God or his own*
*imagination calling him.*
_____  2. *When Abraham heard the Lord tell him to do something that*
*seemed absurd, he immediately dismissed it.*
_____  3. *Isaac apparently shared his father's trust and faith.*

———— 4. *Sacrifice was one means of offering worship to God.*

———— 5. *Like many people of his own time, Abraham believed in human sacrifice.*

———— 6. *Abraham carried out the difficult instructions without questioning.*

# 6 The Lord Will Provide / *Genesis 22:11-18*

Genesis
22:11-13a *At that moment the Angel of God shouted to him from heaven,*
*"Abraham! Abraham!"*

*"Yes, Lord!" he answered.*

*"Lay down the knife; don't hurt the lad in any way," the*
*Angel said, "for I know that God is first in your life—you have*
*not withheld even your beloved son from me."*

*Then Abraham noticed a ram caught by its horns in a bush.*

With relief Abraham laid down the knife, unbound his
son, and bound the ram and laid it on the altar in place of
his son. The father and son did worship together. Abraham
named the place where he had passed this greatest crisis for
his faith *Jehovah-jireh*, meaning "The Lord will provide."

Later generations of God's people comforted
themselves with this saying and they told this story to
encourage themselves in times of greatest crisis, in times
when their own faith was tested. They told the story, too, to
show what kind of a God Jehovah was, a God of mercy, not

a pagan god who wanted them to sacrifice their children, a practice they had seen all too often among other peoples.

How did God reward Abraham for passing this crisis? Really with only a repetition of the promises he had made before—but this time God swore solemnly by himself that he would bring their fulfillment about.

**Genesis 22:15-18**  *Then the Angel of God called again to Abraham from heaven. "I, the Lord, have sworn by myself that because you have obeyed me and have not withheld even your beloved son from me, I will bless you with incredible blessings and multiply your descendants into countless thousands and millions, like the stars above you in the sky, and like the sands along the seashore. These descendants of yours will conquer their enemies, and be a blessing to all the nations of the earth—all because you have obeyed me."*

Abraham never saw any more of a concrete fulfillment of any of these promises except to see his son Isaac grow up, marry, and have twin boys, Jacob and Esau. The Israelites who told these stories after they were settled in the land of Canaan saw themselves as the fulfillment of the promises. But Abraham did not *know* that the promises would be fulfilled. He simply *trusted* that they would be. Abraham could not see how it would all turn out. But his descendants, as they told his story, knew the ending. They themselves were the fulfillment. Abraham's call was now their call. The people of Israel were called to be that multitude of the faithful and to show the power of God to all nations.

The people never forgot Abraham, who so loved God that he was willing to give his own son. Only God himself would ever sacrifice more.

## Getting the Story in Mind

1  *Abraham's relationship with God might best be described as*
_____ *a. controlled by fear of punishment.*
_____ *b. a result of Abraham's sinless life.*
_____ *c. begun by God, continued by Abraham's faithful response.*

2  *The most valuable result of Abraham's faith came in the form of*
_____ *a. a prosperous life.*

_____ *b. prestige among his neighbors.*
_____ *c. promises to be fulfilled in the future.*

3  *We might imagine that the greatest threat Abraham had to face in holding on to his faith was*
_____ *a. ridicule from others.*
_____ *b. a God who was far away.*
_____ *c. unseen promises.*

4  *The greatest lesson to be learned from the life of Abraham is*
_____ *a. God never asks his followers to do anything difficult.*
_____ *b. Friendship with God is worth the sacrifice of anything else.*
_____ *c. It was easier for people to believe in God in the old days.*

5  *If anything would be worth the loss of one's own beloved son, it would be, according to this story,*
_____ *a. victory in war.*
_____ *b. peace and prosperity.*
_____ *c. the reunion of man with God.*

Here are the answers to the questions you have found at the end of each part of
the lesson. Scripture references are provided, where appropriate, to direct
you to the source of the answers.

# 1  Beginning in the Book of Beginnings

*GETTING THE STORY IN MIND*
1   c *(Genesis 3:20, 21)*
2   a *(Genesis 4:1-16)*
3   e *(Genesis 6, 7, 8, 9)*
4   d *(Genesis 11:1-9)*
5   b *(Genesis 12:1-3)*

*GETTING THE MEANING IN HAND*
1   c *(Genesis 1:1)*
2   c *(Genesis 3:22)*
3   c *(Genesis 1:26-28)*
4   c *(Genesis 1:23; 11:4)*
5   b *(Genesis 11:4)*
6   b *(Genesis 11:6)*

# 2  A Good Man Takes a Risk

*GETTING THE STORY IN MIND*
Many Bibles contain maps and atlases. If yours does not, inexpensive maps of
Bible lands can be purchased for a small cost at religious book stores. We
hope you will familiarize yourself with the lands where the biblical
events took place.

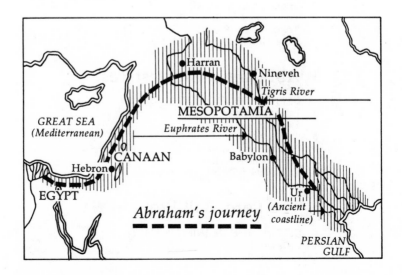

*GETTING THE MEANING IN HAND*
1   b *(Genesis 12:4)*
2   c *(Genesis 12:5)*
3   c *(Genesis 12:6, 7)*
4   a *(Genesis 12–17)*

## 3 Abraham Shows Compassion and Is Rewarded

*GETTING THE STORY IN MIND*
1   a *(Genesis 18:2)*
2   c *(Genesis 18:4-8)*
3   c *(Genesis 18:13-15)*
4   c *(Genesis 18:3-5)*

*GETTING THE MEANING IN HAND*
No one can tell you the answer to this question. You can find the answer only by examining your own life. If, as a result of this lesson, you are able to express compassion for someone you do not know, we'd be happy to hear about it and to share your experience.

## 4 Abraham Negotiates with God

*GETTING THE STORY AND MEANING IN MIND*
1   False *(Genesis 18:17, 18)*
2   True *(Genesis 18:18, 19)*
3   True *(Genesis 18:22)*
4   True *(Genesis 18:23)*
5   True *(Genesis 18:1, 2; 18:22)*
6   False *(Genesis 18:25-33)*
7   True *(Genesis 18:32, 33)*
8   True *(Genesis 18:32)*
9   True *(Genesis 19:13)*
10   False *(Genesis 19:4-6)*

## 5 Abraham's Greatest Test

*GETTING THE STORY IN MIND*
1   False *(Genesis 22:1, 11)*
2   False *(Genesis 22:2, 3)*
3   True *(Genesis 22:7, 8)*
4   True *(Genesis 22:5)*
5   False *(Genesis 22:12)*
6   True *(Genesis 22:10)*

## 6 The Lord Will Provide

*GETTING THE MEANING IN HAND*
1   c *(Genesis 22:16)*
2   c *(Genesis 22:17)*

3   c *(Genesis 22:18)*
4   b *(Genesis 22:18)*
5   c *(Genesis 22:16-18; see also John 3:16)*

## HOW WELL DO YOU KNOW ABRAHAM?

Count your total score on Lesson One:

| | |
|---|---|
| 40-35 correct | You can say you're a close friend of this "friend of God" (James 2:23) |
| 34-30 correct | You're a good friend, though not a close friend. |
| 29-25 correct | You've met him on several occasions. |
| 24-20 correct | You're a passing acquaintance. |
| 19-15 correct | You've barely met the father of the faithful. |
| less than 15 correct | You're still a "stranger." But remember, Abraham was kind to strangers. |

# Part Two

# MOSES

## A People Believes God and Is Rewarded

# 7 How Abraham's Descendants Became Slaves / *Genesis 27–50*

The Israelites often wondered why God had chosen them from among the other nations, particularly when they could see that they were often no better morally than their neighbors. They answered this question by saying they had simply inherited God's gracious blessing as a result of the faith of their fathers, Abraham, Isaac, and Jacob.

The Israelites pointed to two promises God had made to their forefathers. First, God promised Abraham: "I will greatly multiply your descendants." Second, God promised him: "To your descendants I give this land." A people and a land: these promises to Abraham were repeated to his son Isaac and his grandson Jacob.

Through Jacob the first promise of descendants began to take more definite shape, for he had twelve sons. But the promise of a land? Nothing that Jacob had, nothing his sons experienced, nothing that happened to any of the descendants for generations even remotely looked like a gift of land. Instead, Abraham's descendants had become slaves. How did such a discouraging development come about?

Jacob's sons were partly to blame for the fall into slavery. The infighting and jealousy of these twelve brothers foreshadowed the infighting and jealousy that would plague the Israelites for centuries. But there was another influence. God was providing it.

The quarreling brothers, completely unaware of the plans of God, started the fateful events in motion. In a fit of jealousy, they sold one of their number, Jacob's favorite son Joseph, into slavery to a band of merchants headed for Egypt. The story of Joseph and his brothers begins in Genesis chapter 37. It is one of the most vivid and readable narratives in the Bible and in fact, is considered by some contemporary writers to be the first and greatest short story ever written. The entire adventure, from chapter 37 through chapter 45, could be read over a long lunch hour by the busy Bible student. You can learn the bare outlines as you read the rest of our lesson, but there is no substitute for reading the original narrative.

After Joseph labors as a slave, the plan of God begins to unfold. Joseph interprets a strange dream for the royal Egyptian Pharaoh. He is rewarded with the position of minister of agriculture for the whole country. For seven years he is in charge of storing up one-fifth of all the grain grown, preparing for a coming famine, the event Pharaoh had dreamed about.

As the famine sets in, people in outlying regions have to come to Egypt to buy grain. Among the buyers are Joseph's own brothers who come down from Canaan. Joseph recognizes them at once, but of course they are unaware that the stern and mysterious Egyptian administrator is their younger brother. In a suspenseful and agonizing experience for Joseph, as well as for his brothers and their aging father, the family is reconciled once again. The Pharaoh himself invites all of Joseph's family to Egypt:

Genesis 47:11    *So Joseph assigned the best land of Egypt—the land of Rameses—to his father and brothers, just as Pharaoh had commanded.*

The aged Jacob died in Egypt. His sons carried his body back to Canaan, to the family burial place in the cave of

Machpelah, alongside the bones of Abraham and Sarah, Isaac and Rebekah, and Jacob's first wife, Leah. Joseph and his brothers returned to Egypt, where they continued to prosper. In his deathbed will, Joseph gathered his survivors:

Genesis 50:24    *"Soon I will die," Joseph told his brothers, "but God will surely come and get you, and bring you out of this land of Egypt and take you back to the land he promised to the descendants of Abraham, Isaac, and Jacob."*

As the years passed by, the descendants of Joseph and his brothers became a sizable minority group in Egypt. Called "Hebrews" by the Egyptians, they stood out because of their different culture, religion, language, and appearance. Eventually another Pharaoh arose, who the Bible says "knew nothing of Joseph." He began to get a little uneasy about these people. Finally he came up with a policy. When we read the words of his decision, we can't help being struck by the fact that nearly all the prejudices and fears that one group has ever held toward another are found in his words:

Exodus 1:9, 10    *"These Israelis are becoming dangerous to us because there are so many of them. Let's figure out a way to put an end to this. If we don't, and war breaks out, they will join our enemies and fight against us and escape out of the country."*

This forerunner of history's long line of merciless tyrants immediately put his policy into action:

Exodus 1:11    *So the Egyptians made slaves of them and put brutal taskmasters over them to wear them down under heavy burdens while building the store-cities Pithom and Ra-amses.*

But the Pharaoh's plan to reduce the Israelites to an inferior state and keep them there never seemed to work well:

Exodus 1:12-14    *The more the Egyptians mistreated and oppressed them, the more the Israelis seemed to multiply! The Egyptians became alarmed, and made the Hebrew slavery more bitter still, forcing them to toil long and hard in the fields and to carry heavy loads of mortar and brick.*

When this plan failed, the Pharaoh in desperation commanded his army to throw all the newborn male children of the Hebrews into the Nile River. In the midst of this horror and oppression, one baby boy was born who would not be put to death.

## Getting the Story in Mind

On the following page is a "family tree" of people who followed God. Can you trace the course of biblical history? Start at the trunk and work upward shading with your pencil the parts of the tree that figure in the continuing story of divine promise and fulfillment. A look at the Contents page might be of help if you need it.

## Getting the Meaning in Hand

Choose the phrase that best completes the sentence:

1 *The Israelites suffered as slaves in Egypt, because*
_____ *a. God forsook them.*
_____ *b. they rebelled against Pharaoh.*
_____ *c. they were naturally inferior people.*
_____ *d. a tyrannical and prejudiced ruler came to the throne.*

2 *When God chose Israelites to be his people,*
_____ *a. he knew they would keep their side of the covenant.*
_____ *b. he knew they deserved the honor.*
_____ *c. he was keeping a promise.*

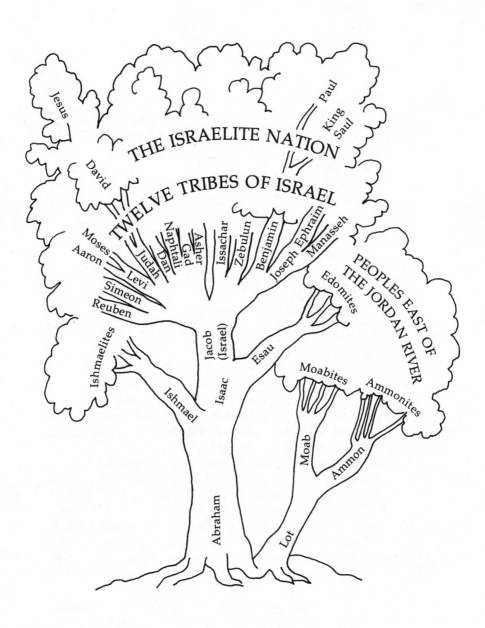

# 8 The Preparation for Freedom Begins / *Exodus 1–4*

Exodus
2:1-10 *There were at this time a Hebrew fellow and girl of the tribe of Levi who married and had a family, and a baby son was born to them. When the baby's mother saw that he was an unusually beautiful baby, she hid him at home for three months. Then, when she could no longer hide him, she made a little boat from papyrus reeds, waterproofed it with tar, put the baby in it, and laid it among the reeds along the river's edge. The baby's sister watched from a distance to see what would happen to him.*

*Well, this is what happened: A princess, one of Pharaoh's daughters, came down to bathe in the river, and as she and her maids were walking along the river bank, she spied the little boat among the reeds and sent one of the maids to bring it to her. When she opened it, there was a baby! And he was crying. This touched her heart. "He must be one of the Hebrew children!" she said.*

*Then the baby's sister approached the princess and asked her, "Shall I go and find one of the Hebrew women to nurse the baby for you?"*

*"Yes, do!" the princess replied. So the little girl rushed home and called her mother!*

*"Take this child home and nurse him for me," the princess instructed the baby's mother, "and I will pay you well!" So she took him home and nursed him.*

*Later, when he was older, she brought him back to the princess and he became her son. She named him Moses (meaning "to draw out") because she had drawn him out of the water.*

Against the standing order of the king to kill all infant Hebrew males, Pharaoh's daughter herself violated the rule. As a result, the young Moses was reared in the royal palace, presumably with all the advantages of a princely Egyptian education. This education obviously did not include training for faith in the God of Abraham, Isaac, and Jacob. Was his mother able to convey this faith in God and solidarity with his people in the short time she nursed him? Somehow he gained identity with his own people, and sided with them in the face of their oppression. As a young man Moses killed an Egyptian—secretly, he thought—when he saw the man beating an Israelite.

Discovering that the secret was out, Moses had to escape. He fled north and east to the Midian wilderness in the Sinai Peninsula. There he stayed with a rugged sheep-herding tribe, marrying Zipporah, the daughter of the local high priest, and settling into the primitive life of a shepherd.

For a young man accustomed to Egyptian royal palace living, minding a flock of aimless and straying sheep must have seemed boring and pointless. Little did he know how the experience might prepare him for leading a multitude of aimless and straying people.

During the hours and months and years of boredom, one day Moses' life was changed instantly, in a moment of terror and awe. Out in the wilderness he saw a bush on fire.

Exodus 3:2b-8a

*When Moses saw that the bush was on fire and that it didn't burn up, he went over to investigate. Then God called out to him, "Moses! Moses!"*

*"Who is it?" Moses asked.*

*"Don't come any closer," God told him. "Take off your shoes,*

*for you are standing on holy ground. I am the God of your fathers—the God of Abraham, Isaac, and Jacob." (Moses covered his face with his hands, for he was afraid to look at God.)*

*Then the Lord told him, "I have seen the deep sorrows of my people in Egypt, and have heard their pleas for freedom from their harsh taskmasters. I have come to deliver them from the Egyptians and to take them out of Egypt into a good land, a large land.*

The forces are gathering for one of the great events in history. Moses is told the part he will play:

Exodus 3:10    *"Now I am going to send you to Pharaoh, to demand that he let you lead my people out of Egypt."*

Moses is overwhelmed. His response is a barrage of questions and excuses: "I'm not the person for a job like that." "What shall I tell them?" "But they won't believe me." "O Lord, I'm just not a good speaker." "Lord, please! Send someone else." At this point, the main idea in Moses' prayer is "Lord, send anybody you want to—except me."

## Getting the Story in Mind

Check the best ending for the following statements.

1 *Moses was born into the Israelite tribe of*
_____ *a. Levi, the tribe of priests.*
_____ *b. Judah, the tribe of kings.*
_____ *c. Ephraim and Manasseh, tribes of Joseph's sons.*

2 *Moses' mother laid him in a waterproof basket and set him floating on*
_____ *a. the Jordan River.*
_____ *b. the Euphrates River.*
_____ *c. the Nile River.*

3 *When Pharaoh's daughter came to bathe in the river and she found the Hebrew baby floating in the river, she*
_____ *a. threw him into the water in obedience to her father's command.*
_____ *b. told her father about the baby.*
_____ *c. secretly rescued him.*

4 Pharaoh's daughter unknowingly hired, as Moses' nurse,
_____ a. his sister.
_____ b. his mother.
_____ c. his palace servant.

5 When Moses grew up, he took sides with
_____ a. the oppressed Hebrew people.
_____ b. the Egyptian royal family.
_____ c. the foreign enemies who threatened the Egyptian boundaries.

6 When Moses found out that the people knew he had killed an Egyptian,
_____ a. he begged Pharaoh for forgiveness.
_____ b. he went to the Israelites for protection.
_____ c. he fled into the Sinai desert.

7 Among the Midianite sheep-herders, Moses
_____ a. tried to raise an army to go back and free his people from Egyptian bondage.
_____ b. lived a life of leisure befitting an Egyptian prince in exile.
_____ c. married a daughter of the local high priest and helped him herd sheep.

8 Moses' long years herding sheep was, for a man of his talents,
_____ a. a waste of time.
_____ b. a way to get rich.
_____ c. a preparation for a future vocation.

9 When Moses saw the burning bush, he
_____ a. tried to put it out.
_____ b. ran away in terror.
_____ c. approached it cautiously.

10 When God told Moses to go free his people, he immediately
_____ a. agreed to do it.
_____ b. began to make excuses.
_____ c. flatly refused.

## Getting the Meaning in Hand

Despite the unique features of Moses' life—the little river basket, the burning bush, for example—his development and growth followed a pattern that is common to most of us. On the left are some of the stages that psychologists say

people go through on their way from childhood through
adolescence to maturity. Match the events in Moses' life to
these stages.

_____ 1. *Childhood values received*     _____ a. *burning bush*
           *in the home.*
_____ 2. *Formal knowledge acquired*     _____ b. *slaying of*
           *through schooling*                        *Egyptian*
_____ 3. *Early attempts to define*      _____ c. *living in the*
           *goals end in failure.*                   *palace*
_____ 4. *Period of aimlessness,*        _____ d. *Mother serves*
           *incubation.*                              *as nurse*
_____ 5. *Flash of insight when*         _____ e. *herding sheep*
           *motivation is received to*               *in the desert*
           *pursue one's life goals.*

## Side Trip

Has your life and your vocation followed the process outlined
above, at least approximately? Make a note of some of the
experiences of your life that correspond to each of the
stages.

# 9 The First Attempts End in Failure / Exodus 4–6

Moses had some very real and practical fears about becoming the deliverer of his people. Nevertheless, to all Moses' questions, the answer of the Lord is the same:

Exodus 3:6 (15, 16; 4:5)

*"I am the God of your fathers—the God of Abraham, Isaac, and Jacob."*

The God who appears to Moses is no gray abstraction. He is not a projection of Moses' imagination, nor a sentimental memory from childhood. He is the eternal, living God. He has acted in the past. He is acting in the present. He will act in the future. He is merciful. He is powerful. Moses realizes that if he puts his trust in this God, he will find assurance to take away his fears and doubts.

Ready to take the risk of following the Lord's will, Moses and his family leave the familiar surroundings of Midian and head south for the dangerous and oppressive land of Egypt. Like his forefather Abraham, Moses is willing to give up the comfort and security of home to follow the Lord, even if it means hardship and trouble. He would rather be with the Lord in a life of struggle than to be without him in a life of ease. This characteristic will mark every one of God's people throughout history down to the 20th century.

Moses was not long in Egypt before the time came for him to confront Pharaoh. He approached the throne and made a single nonnegotiable demand:

Exodus 5:1   *"We bring you a message from Jehovah, the God of Israel. He says, 'Let my people go, for they must make a holy pilgrimage out into the wilderness, for a religious feast, to worship me there.' "*

Was Pharaoh impressed? He was hardly the kind of man to roll over and play dead at the words of an unknown sheepherder.

Exodus 5:2   *"Is that so?" retorted Pharaoh. "And who is Jehovah, that I should listen to him, and let Israel go? I don't know Jehovah and I will not let Israel go."*

This might have crushed a man who was not trusting God to work things out. Pharaoh roared his indignation:

Exodus 5:4, 5   *"Who do you think you are," Pharaoh shouted, "distracting the people from their work? Get back to your jobs!"*

Pharaoh's answer to the demand for freedom was to make things worse for the slaves. He would make their work quota harder to reach. No longer would their straw be supplied for brickmaking; they would have to gather it themselves. When they failed to meet their quota, they would be whipped. Some of the slaves went to Pharaoh, this time without Moses, to complain. He turned them away:

Exodus 5:17, 18   *"You don't have enough work, or else you wouldn't be saying, 'Let us go and sacrifice to Jehovah.' Get back to work. No straw will be given you, and you must deliver the regular quota of bricks."*

Pharaoh hoped to drive a wedge between the slaves and their

new leaders, and it looked as if his strategy might work. The
slaves who had gone to Pharaoh returned to the camp and
accused Moses and his brother Aaron:

Exodus
5:21

*"May God judge you for making us stink before Pharaoh and his
people," they said, "and for giving them an excuse to kill us."*

Instead of arguing with them, Moses turns to God. He
pours out his doubts and feelings of frustration:

Exodus
5:22, 23

*"Lord," he protested, "how can you mistreat your own people
like this? Why did you ever send me, if you were going to do this to
them? Ever since I gave Pharaoh your message, he has only
been more and more brutal to them, and you have not delivered
them at all!"*

In Moses' eyes, he is falling behind in the contest with
Pharaoh, and that worries him. God's answer is to point
him away from the early defeats to the eventual victory:

Exodus
6:6-9

...*"I will use my mighty power and perform great miracles to
deliver them from slavery, and make them free. And I will accept
them as my people and be their God. And they shall know that I
am Jehovah their God who has rescued them from the
Egyptians. I will bring them into the land I promised to give to
Abraham, Isaac, and Jacob. It shall belong to my people."*

With the evidence of what God has done in the past, with
the promise of what he will do in the future, Moses is able
to trust God in the crisis of the present.

## Getting the Story in Mind

Mark the following statements *True* or *False.*

_____ 1. *Moses was eager to confront Pharaoh.*
_____ 2. *Moses and the people had to trust God's promise that he would
be with him.*
_____ 3. *Pharaoh, impressed with Moses' speech, allowed the Israelites
to leave immediately.*
_____ 4. *After hearing Moses' demand, Pharaoh punished the Israelites
with a heavier work load.*

_____ 5. The Israelite slaves thanked Moses for trying to help them.
_____ 6. The Israelite slaves blamed Moses for their heavier work load.
_____ 7. Moses was afraid to talk to God about his failure to free the people.
_____ 8. Moses complained to God that God had done nothing to help his people.
_____ 9. God told Moses to give up trying to free the people, because Pharaoh was too stubborn.
_____ 10. God told Moses to keep on trying to free the people because Pharaoh would finally let them go.

## Getting the Meaning in Hand

Check the phrase that best completes the sentence:

1 Life with God led the slaves to hope for
_____ a. immediate results.
_____ b. ultimate peace and freedom.
_____ c. meaningless toil and drudgery.

2 When faced with the crisis of failure, Moses
_____ a. tries to cover it up.
_____ b. expresses his feelings to God.
_____ c. charges on as if nothing serious happened.

## Defining God's Promises

The Lord makes five promises to his people (Exodus 6:6-8). To understand better what each of these promises actually means, match the dictionary definitions on the right with the word of promise on the left.

_____ 1. "I will deliver them."        a. to receive with favor

_____ 2. "I will rescue them."         b. to cause to come with oneself by leading or conveying

_____ 3. "I will make them free."      c. to set at liberty, to liberate

_____ 4. "I will accept them."         d. to free from bondage

_____ 5. "I will bring them."          e. to seize from any confinement, danger, evil

# 10 Escape to Freedom / *Exodus 7–15*

A man like Pharaoh, who could permit the brutality and injustice that the Israelites suffered, was not the kind of man who would listen to reason or appeals to the conscience. God told Moses, "In the end Pharaoh will let them go." But God also told Moses it would take a show of force: "I will redeem you with arm outstretched and with mighty acts of judgment."

Pharaoh had some hard lessons to learn. He was going to have to discover that the God of Abraham, Isaac, and Jacob was also Creator of heaven and earth, of rivers and lands, of plants and animals, of life and death.

An awesome display of power and destruction begins. The River Nile is turned to blood. Pharaoh promises to let the people go if God will make the water safe to drink again. The people prepare to escape to freedom. The blood turns back to water. Pharaoh changes his mind.

Swarms of frogs appear on the land. Pharaoh promises. The people get ready. God destroys the frogs. Pharaoh backs down. When the frogs die, maggots appear, then flies. Then the Egyptian cattle die. The people get terrible boils. Through each of the plagues Pharaoh keeps up his strategy of making promises to get rid of the torment, only to renege when he gets his way. A hailstorm beats down the crops. An engulfing cloud of locusts, blown in by the roaring east wind, destroys the crops and blots out the sun. A thick darkness covers the earth for three days. Pharaoh bargains and blusters his way through it all, power politics at its best.

But God had prepared yet another "mighty act of judgment." This one, God tells the people, will break the Pharaoh's resistance. To demonstrate their faith, the people were told to celebrate the victory in *advance!* They were told to prepare a feast. They were to kill a lamb or young goat, and to sprinkle its blood upon the doorposts and lintels of their houses. Then they were to roast and eat the lamb with unleavened bread and bitter herbs. Other very detailed instructions were commanded by God. For an enslaved people who had yet to see a single one of the "mighty acts" subdue the heart of Pharaoh, the eating of this victory feast, in advance, stands as one of the great acts of faith and obedience in human history.

But eat it they did. The celebration became known as the "Feast of the Passover" because of the event that occurred later in the night. It happened as God had revealed it to Moses:

Exodus 11:4-7a   *"About midnight I will pass through Egypt. And all the oldest sons shall die in every family in Egypt, from the oldest child of Pharaoh, heir to his throne, to the oldest child of his lowliest slave; and even the firstborn of the animals. The wail of death will resound throughout the entire land of Egypt; never before has there been such anguish, and it will never be again.*

*"But not a dog shall move his tongue against any of the people of Israel, nor shall any of their animals die."*

The Bible records that Pharaoh summoned Moses and Aaron while it was still night and said:

Exodus 12:31, 32   *"Leave us; please go away, all of you; go and serve Jehovah as you said. Take your flocks and herds and be gone; and oh, give me a blessing as you go."*

The Israelites fled in the night, taking all they could carry
with them. Led by Moses and Aaron, the great throng of
slaves went out, not knowing where they were headed. They
had only a dream and a promise God had made in
connection with their feast:

Exodus     *"When you come into the land that the Lord will give you, just as*
12:25-27  *he promised, and when you are celebrating the Passover, and your*
*children ask, 'What does all this mean? What is this ceremony*
*about?' you will reply, 'It is the celebration of Jehovah's*
*passing over us, for he passed over the homes of the people of*
*Israel, though he killed the Egyptians; he passed over our houses*
*and did not come in to destroy us.' "*

In the course of their journey the Israelites approached the
sea that separated them from the Sinai wilderness which
they were to enter. By this time Pharaoh's grief had worn off,
and the loss of all that free labor began to soak in. True to form,
he came after the freed slaves with rumbling chariots.
    When the Israelites saw the stretch of water ahead of
them, the cloud of dust from the chariots behind them, they
did what any normal multitude would do. They panicked:

Exodus     *"And they turned against Moses, whining, "Have you brought*
14:11    *us out here to die in the desert because there were not enough*
*graves for us in Egypt?"*

If the truly faithful man would rather be with God in a life of
struggle than to be without him in a life of ease, the Israelites
at this point were just the opposite. They preferred slavery
*without* God to freedom *with* him:

Exodus    *"Why did you make us leave Egypt? Isn't this what we told you,*
14:11b, 12  *while we were slaves, to leave us alone? We said it would be better*
*to be slaves to the Egyptians than dead in the wilderness."*

At this moment of terror, Moses stands as a tower of faith:

Exodus    *"Don't be afraid. Just stand where you are and watch, and you*
14:13    *will see the wonderful way the Lord will rescue you today."*

What happened next is one of the most familiar and

dramatic events in the Bible. Moses raises his staff over the water. A strong east wind turns the sea-bed into dry land. The Israelites cross, but as Pharaoh's charioteers try to follow, their wheels become hopelessly mired. The sea flows back into its normal channels and they cannot escape.

Safe on the other side, freed from bondage, and seeing victory for the first time, the Israelites break into singing:

Exodus
15:1

*I will sing to the Lord, for he has triumphed gloriously;*
*He has thrown both horse and rider into the sea.*

Not very impressive lyrics, perhaps, compared to some of the other psalms and hymns in the Bible. But the song was a sign of a great breakthrough: the people were learning to praise the Lord.

## Getting the Story in Mind

Below are listed some events retold in our story above, but in scrambled order. Can you place the events in the order in which they happened? Write the letter of the first event by the number 1, the second event by the number 2, and so on.

1. _____ *a. Pharaoh frees the Israelite slaves.*
2. _____ *b. Israelites celebrate the first Passover feast.*
3. _____ *c. Nine plagues come to the land of Egypt.*
4. _____ *d. Israelites pass through the sea on dry land.*
5. _____ *e. Pharaoh still refuses to let the people go.*
6. _____ *f. Pharaoh and his army pursue the fleeing slaves.*
7. _____ *g. Death strikes all first-born Egyptians.*
8. _____ *h. The Egyptian charioteers are drowned in the sea.*
9. _____ *i. The Israelites sing their first praise song to God in the Wilderness.*

## Getting the Meaning in Hand

Check the phrase that best completes the sentence:

1 *To celebrate the victory over Pharaoh in advance of the event shows*

_____ *a. the people were overanxious and easy to impress.*
_____ *b. they were sticking only with the facts.*
_____ *c. they were taking a risk of faith.*

2 *The Passover meal was observed through the centuries*
_____ *a. to celebrate God's love and power on their behalf.*
_____ *b. because the people loved elaborate rituals.*
_____ *c. as a sentimental custom.*
_____ *d. because it was always done that way.*

3 *"Saved by the blood of the lamb" was an idea that pointed to*
_____ *a. God's mercy on behalf of man's weakness.*
_____ *b. a crude, primitive Jewish rite.*
_____ *c. an experience only peoples long ago could understand.*
_____ *d. an experience only peoples of today can understand.*

# 11 The Slaves Learn About Citizenship / *Exodus 16–40*

Now that the threat of Pharaoh's army was dead, the tumultuous band of freed slaves made their way through the wilderness of Sinai. It was familiar territory to Moses. Not far away lay the land of Midian where he had spent years as a shepherd. The long hot days minding flocks of straying sheep would have given him invaluable experience.

The Israelites had a lot to learn. Through the generations of slavery their initiative had been systematically destroyed. They had little or no opportunity for schooling. Contact with their heritage from Abraham, Isaac, and Jacob was all but forgotten. And, of course, their forefathers were not free from strife and infighting, as the twelve sons of Jacob clearly proved. For slaves who longed for the security of life under Pharaoh, there was a long, tough road ahead to genuine freedom as the divine plan intended it for them.

So for the next forty years Moses led the people in the wilderness. They would have to learn first of all to depend

upon God for survival. In the deserts of Sinai they had to
look to God even for their food and drink, and that usually a
day at a time.

While the story reveals the Israelites waiting forty years
to get their bearings in the wilderness, it is well for us to
pause in this story to get our own bearings.

The narrative that leads us from the beginnings to
Abraham, Isaac, Jacob, and Joseph is contained in the Book of
*Genesis*. The continuation of that story after the
descendants of Joseph have fallen into slavery is
contained in the Book of *Exodus*. Indeed, "exodus" means
exit or deliverance. The two books of Genesis and Exodus are
powerful and moving; on one level as exciting narrative, on a
higher level as inspiring revelation of the purposes of God
with men. On both levels countless men and women of all
walks of life have read these two books again and again. So
it often comes as a shock to the unwary to turn the page from
the last chapter of Exodus to the first chapter of Leviticus. The
narrative breaks off. The books of Leviticus, Numbers, and
Deuteronomy are quite detailed and more difficult to
follow.

In a quick survey course like this one, we will only
summarize the contents—coming up in the next part. The
story of the wandering Israelites, on their way to the
promised land, picks up again in the book of Joshua.

With these caution signs posted, we can return to the
book of Exodus.

In the course of their wilderness wanderings, the Israelites
reached Mount Sinai, the place where the Lord had earlier
appeared to Moses out of a burning bush, revealing his
power and holiness, his love and faithfulness. In this same
mountain the Lord now reveals himself to his people. As he
had done with their forefathers, God offers to bind himself
with a special agreement called a covenant. He will be their
God; they will be his people. In this covenant God makes
certain promises and asks certain responses:

Exodus
19:4-6
*"You have seen what I did to the Egyptians, and how I brought
you to myself as though on eagle's wings. Now if you will obey me
and keep your part of my contract with you, you shall be my
own little flock from among all the nations of the earth; for all*

*the earth is mine. And you shall be a kingdom of priests to God, a holy nation."*

A "kingdom of priests," a "holy nation"—how these ideals must have staggered the imagination of this band of slaves! But they had faith to enter into the covenant, saying, "We will obey, and do all that the Lord has said." The heart of the covenant came in the form of Ten Commandments: four commandments dealing with the love and service of God; six dealing with the love and service of their fellow men.

With the best of intentions the Israelites consented to the covenant. Scarcely had they finished their vows when, in a frenzy of primitive ecstasy, they broke them.

## Getting the Story in Mind

Mark the following statements *True* or *False*.

_____ 1. *After the Israelites escaped from Egypt, they marched straight into the promised land.*

_____ 2. *The Israelites wandered in the desert for forty years before entering the promised land.*

_____ 3. *When life grew hard in the wilderness, the Israelites often wished they were back in Egypt.*

_____ 4. *While in the wilderness, the Israelites had to depend upon God for their food a day at a time.*

_____ 5. *At Mount Sinai God made a covenant with the Israelites.*

_____ 6. *In his covenant with the Israelites, God made promises to them but no demands upon them.*

_____ 7. *The people as a whole received no evidence of God's presence.*

_____ 8. *When the Israelites first heard the laws of the covenant, they refused to agree to them.*

_____ 9. *The Ten Commandments concern love and service to God and to one's neighbor.*

_____ 10. *The Israelites kept the commandments faithfully throughout their experience in the wilderness.*

## Getting the Meaning in Hand

The Ten Commandments (Exodus 20) were intended to guide the Israelites in all their beliefs and actions. Some Commandments are related to God, some to self, some to family, some to neighbor. Match the descriptions on the right to the Ten Commandments on the left:

_____ 1. You may worship no other god than me.

_____ 2. You shall not make yourselves any idols: any images resembling animals, birds, or fish.

_____ 3. You shall not use the name of Jehovah irreverently.

_____ 4. Remember to observe the Sabbath as a holy day.

_____ 5. Honor your father and mother.

_____ 6. You must not murder.

_____ 7. You must not commit adultery.

_____ 8. You must not steal.

_____ 9. You must not lie.

_____ 10. You must not be envious.

a. the commandment against worshiping material objects.

b. the commandment concerning the unity and oneness of God.

c. the commandment that recognizes man's need for rest, refreshment, and reflection on God

d. the commandment aganist trivializing the name of God

e. the commandment of respect for the family as the fundamental unity of society.

f. the commandment that shows the sacredness of sex in marriage.

g. the commandment that prohibits scheming to get rich at the expense of others.

h. the commandment that affirms the sanctity of human life.

i. the commandment that demands honesty and justice in the community.

j. the commandment that views a man's property as an extension of his own soul or self.

# 12 The People Learn About Worship and Morality / *Leviticus, Numbers, Deuteronomy*

As great leaders often must do, Moses had to get away from his people on occasion, to get his own spiritual batteries recharged. With the people camped below, Moses retreated high atop Mount Sinai to commune with God, and to receive God's latest message for his people.

Moses had been away for about a month when the people started to worry whether he was ever coming down again. An invisible God, an absent leader, nothing to do; the tension was too much. They talked Aaron into making them a new god that they could see and control. A golden calf—that was good enough for the neighboring peoples and good enough for them! With the revelry and abandonment typical of pagan calf worship, the people were hardly aware when Moses returned to their midst.

Bearing new tablets of stone inscribed with the laws of the covenant, Moses viewed the orgiastic sight in horror. Smashing the tablets to the ground, he warned the people that a dreadful punishment would come.

Moses ascended the mountain for another forty days and received the covenant anew. This time, upon his return, the contrite people busied themselves in constructing the tent of meeting, or tabernacle, according to God's instructions.

The covenant between God and Israel was intended as a system of justice. The tabernacle was intended as a means of worship. The laws and instructions that fill the books of *Leviticus, Numbers* and *Deuteronomy* address every situation that was likely to be met by a group of slaves trying, with God's help, to become "a kingdom of priests," "a holy nation." Even a brief skimming of these laws and instructions reveals how down to earth they were. Many are obscure and inapplicable today, of course. But behind each of the rules were two basic principles: love of God and love of neighbor.

There was no part of life where these principles did not apply. Health, farming, child care, funerals, festivals, marriage, schooling, sewage disposal—all of life was to be governed by love of God and love of neighbor. Of particular importance was treatment of the poor, of the stranger, of the weak. Israel was once poor, weak, and in a strange land; God had shown mercy and compassion to them. Now they must do the same to one another.

The final message of Moses, as revealed through the speeches in the book of Deuteronomy, pled for faithfulness to God and justice to fellow man. Whenever the Israelites turn from God to worship a creation of stone or gold, whenever they turn from compassion to neglect, they will surely be punished, warned Moses. Their promises, he predicted, would be fulfilled only if they were faithful.

Although Moses led his people for forty years, he was not among those who actually got to the promised land. After standing on a mountain to take one last, long, wistful look into the beautiful country, Moses died. The Bible says that God himself buried Moses where no one could find him, perhaps an indication that his people should look forward to God's continuing plans, not backward with misplaced veneration.

Among the heroes of Israelite faith, Moses towers as one of the greatest:

Deuteronomy 34:10

*There has never been another prophet like Moses, for the Lord talked to him face to face.*

## Getting the Story in Mind

Use the words listed here to fill in the blanks below. Caution: there are some extra words.

| | | |
|---|---|---|
| *tabernacle* | *neglect* | *king* |
| *Aaron* | *Sinai* | *tablets* |
| *love* | *Zipporah* | *tolerate* |
| *prophet* | *temple* | *Ararat* |

1  *Moses went to the top of Mount _____ to commune with God.*

2  *While Moses was gone, his brother _____ made the people a golden calf to worship.*

3  *When Moses saw the people worshiping the image, he smashed the stone _____ inscribed with the law.*

4  *When Moses returned a second time, the people busied themselves making the tent of God or _____ .*

5  *Behind the many laws in Exodus, Leviticus, Numbers, and Deuteronomy was the principle of _____ for God and one's neighbor.*

6  *God's covenant demanded the Israelites not _____ the poor and weak and the strangers among them.*

7  *Although Moses was a great _____ he died before he led his people into the promised land.*

On the left are listed the first five books of the Bible. On the right are descriptions of the contents of the books. Often in the description there is a word similar to the name of the books. Match each description with the correct book by placing the correct letter beside each number.

| | | |
|---|---|---|
| _____ | 1. *Genesis* | a. *second giving of the law* |
| _____ | 2. *Exodus* | b. *census of the people* |
| _____ | 3. *Leviticus* | c. *Israelites exit from Egypt* |
| _____ | 4. *Numbers* | d. *duties for Levite priests* |
| _____ | 5. *Deuteronomy* | e. *a book of beginnings* |

## Getting the Meaning in Hand

*Freedom Songs.* Down through the centuries, people keep
turning again and again to the redemption from slavery,
the wilderness wandering and the promised land, as
descriptions of their own life and experience. Many
psalms, hymns and spirituals that are familiar to millions are
based on these events. Match the lettered events with the
numbered hymn lyrics below:

_____ 1. *"Go down, Moses, 'way down in Egypt land...."*
_____ 2. *"On Jordan's stormy banks I stand and cast a wistful eye...."*
_____ 3. *"Guide me, O thou great Jehovah, pilgrim through this barren
            land...."*
_____ 4. *"Our father's God, to thee, author of liberty, to thee we
            sing...."*
_____ 5. *"To thee, whose blood can cleanse each spot, O lamb of God, I
            come...."*
_____ 6. *"I'm just a poor wayfaring stranger...."*
_____ 7. *"Before I'd be a slave, I'd be buried in my grave...."*

    *a. the evils of slavery*
    *b. the sacrificial lamb*
    *c. God's commission to Moses*
    *d. God's act of liberty*
    *e. God guides the people through the wilderness*
    *f. the people wander in a strange land*
    *g. the people prepare to cross over the river into Canaan*

Here are the answers to the questions you have found at the end of each part of this lesson. Scripture references are provided to direct you to the source of the answers.

## 7 How Abraham's Descendants Became Slaves

*GETTING THE STORY IN MIND*
*Score one point for each of the following areas you shaded: Abraham, Isaac, Jacob, twelve sons, Moses-Aaron, David-Jesus, Benjamin-Paul. Subtract one point for each area you shaded in addition to these.*

*GETTING THE MEANING IN HAND*
1   d *(Genesis 37:1-36; Genesis 42-50; Exodus 1:8-12)*
2   c *(Exodus 6:2-8)*

## 8 The Preparation for Freedom Begins

*GETTING THE STORY IN MIND*
1   a *(Exodus 2:1)*
2   c *(Exodus 2:3; 1:22)*
3   c *(Exodus 2:5-10)*
4   b *(Exodus 2:7, 8)*
5   a *(Exodus 2:11)*
6   c *(Exodus 2:15)*
7   c *(Exodus 2:16-22)*
8   c *(Exodus 2:23-25)*
9   c *(Exodus 3:1-5)*
10   b *(Exodus 3:10; 4:17)*

*GETTING THE MEANING IN HAND*
1   d *(Exodus 2:9, 10)*
2   c *(Exodus 2:11)*
3   b *(Exodus 2:11-15)*
4   e *(Exodus 2:21)*
5   a *(Exodus 3:1-10)*

## 9 The First Attempts End in Failure

*GETTING THE STORY IN MIND*
1   False *(Exodus 3:10; 4:17)*
2   True *(Exodus 4:29-31)*
3   False *(Exodus 5:2)*
4   True *(Exodus 5:6-8)*
5   False *(Exodus 5:20)*
6   True *(Exodus 5:21)*
7   False *(Exodus 5:22)*
8   True *(Exodus 5:23)*
9   False *(Exodus 6:1)*
10   True *(Exodus 6:6)*

*GETTING THE MEANING IN HAND*
1   b *(Exodus 6:6-8)*
2   b *(Exodus 5:22, 23)*

*Defining God's Promises*
1   c
2   e
3   d
4   a
5   b
     For more understanding of these promises, look up the five terms in a dictionary, or better, a Bible encyclopedia, dictionary, or concordance.

## 10   Escape to Freedom

*GETTING THE STORY IN MIND*
The sentences should be numbered as follows:
1   c *(Exodus 7, 8, 9, 10)*
2   e *(Exodus 10:27, 28)*
3   b *(Exodus 12:1-28)*
4   g *(Exodus 12:29, 30)*
5   a *(Exodus 12:31, 32)*
6   f *(Exodus 14:5-8)*
7   d *(Exodus 14:21, 22)*
8   h *(Exodus 14:23-29)*
9   i *(Exodus 15:1-18)*

*GETTING THE MEANING IN HAND*
1   c *(Exodus 12:28)*
2   a *(Exodus 12:25-27)*
3   a *(Exodus 12:13; 12:17; 12:23)*

## 11   The Slaves Learn about Citizenship

*GETTING THE STORY IN MIND*
1   False *(Numbers 14:33)*
2   True *(Numbers 14:34)*
3   True *(Exodus 16:3; 17:3; Numbers 14:1-3)*
4   True *(Exodus 16:11-21; 16:31-35)*
5   True *(Exodus 19:1-7, especially 19:2, 5, 6)*
6   False *(Exodus 19:7, 8)*
7   False *(Exodus 19:9; 19:16-19)*
8   False *(Exodus 19:5)*
9   True *(Exodus 20:1-17)*
10   False *(Exodus 32:1-10, especially 32:8)*

*GETTING THE MEANING IN HAND*
The Ten Commandments are found in their more complete form in Exodus Chapter 20.
1   b
2   a
3   d
4   c
5   e

6  h
7  f
8  j
9  i
10  g

## 12 The People Learn about Worship and Morality

*GETTING THE STORY IN MIND*
Fill in the blanks:
1  Sinai *(Exodus 24:15-18)*
2  Aaron *(Exodus 32:1-4)*
3  tablets *(Exodus 32:19)*
4  tabernacle *(Exodus 35:10, 29)*
5  love *(Deuteronomy 6:4, 5; Leviticus 19:18)*
6  neglect *(Exodus 23:9; Leviticus 19:9-14)*
7  prophet *(Deuteronomy 34:10)*

Finding your way around:
1  e *(Genesis 1:1)*
2  c *(Exodus 12:30-35)*
3  d *(the word "priest" occurs 175 times in Leviticus, nearly half the occurrences in the entire Old Testament)*
4  b *(Numbers 1:2)*
5  a *(Deuteronomy 5:1; from Greek words for second ["deutero"] and law ["nemos"]*

*GETTING THE MEANING IN HAND*
**Freedom Songs**
1  c
2  g
3  f or e
4  d
5  b
6  e or f
7  a

## *ARE YOU KEEPING UP WITH THE ISRAELITES?*
It's been a long, uphill struggle out of Egypt, through the wilderness, to the edge of the promised land. Gauge your progress by this scale:

| | |
|---|---|
| 80-93 correct | You're on the banks of the promised land! |
| 70-79 correct | Look up! River Jordan just ahead. |
| 60-69 correct | You're still wandering in the wilderness. |
| 50-59 correct | You're safe from Pharaoh, but your journey's just beginning. |
| 40-49 correct | Hurry! The waters are falling back into the sea. |
| below 40 correct | Sorry, Pharaoh's got you. |

Whether your score is high or low, a verse from the next lesson is instructive:
*The Lord does not see as man sees; men judge by appearances, but the Lord judges by the heart.* (1 Samuel 16:7)

# Part Three

# DAVID

## A Man Opposes God and Is Restored

# 13 After Moses, A Time of Violence / *Joshua, Judges*

Moses, the wise, patient, trusting leader, the man who gave his people the law of God, and who pled his people's case before their God, would be replaced by a quite different kind of leader with a quite different kind of task. Moses' successor, Joshua, was a military man. Moses had led his people through forty years of preparation for entering the promised land, but Joshua would be the one to take them in.

Joshua is well known, of course, in connection with the Battle of Jericho, the city whose "walls came a-tumblin' down." This battle was one in a series the Israelites had to fight in taking possession of their land. Joshua is rightly identified with the most violent and bloody period of the Bible.

The wars of utter destruction, wars the Israelites were divinely commanded to fight, are one of the most difficult parts of the Bible to understand. People have gone to two tragic extremes in trying to understand the wars of the

Israelites. Some have turned from the biblical faith in anger, justifying their rejection by saying that the biblical view of God as a commanding general is bloodthirsty, uncivilized, immoral. Others have headed in the other direction, trying to prove their own wars are sanctioned by God like the conquests described in the Bible. Many of history's bloodiest battles have been between opponents who both believed that God was on their side.

Even with all the fighting, the Israelites gained only a foothold in the promised land. In many cases, they simply had to move in next door to the native peoples. The twelve tribes were scattered throughout the land and separated from one another by rivers, hills, and enemy territory. They had no strong political organization. The tribes were held together principally by their faith. They all worshiped God at a central shrine in the city of Shiloh. There had been placed the Ark of the Covenant, a small, beautiful box containing relics from their exodus and their wanderings, to remind them that God had led them, that they had not been delivered on their own.

Near the end of his life, Joshua made a farewell address similar to that of Moses. As long as the people would live faithfully, Joshua said, they would prosper. If they ever forgot God and their fellow man, and wandered after idols and injustice, a multitude of troubles would overtake them.

After Joshua died, the twelve tribes had no official leaders for many years, only judges who settled disputes and led occasional forays against their aggressive neighbors. Among these judges were Gideon, who routed an army of thousands with 300 men; Deborah, the woman general; Samson, protector against the Philistines. But the most important judge was Samuel. He would preside over Israel as it passed into its Golden Age.

## Getting the Story in Mind

Mark the following statements *True* or *False*.

_____ 1. *Moses led his people out of the wilderness into the promised land.*

_____ 2. *After Joshua fought the Battle of Jericho, there were still more cities for the Israelites to conquer.*

_____  3. The Israelites themselves planned all their own battle strategy while fighting for the land of Canaan.

_____  4. When the Israelites moved into Canaan, they did not kill all of the native inhabitants.

_____  5. As soon as they moved into Canaan, the Israelites chose a king to govern them.

_____  6. Although scattered throughout the land, the Israelites worshiped God at a central shrine in Shiloh.

_____  7. Once God had fulfilled his promise to give them the land, the Israelites didn't need to worry about keeping their side of the covenant.

_____  8. During their early years in Canaan, the Israelites were governed by judges.

# 14 The People Demand a Ruler
## *1 Samuel 1–16*

Life in the promised land was full of hardship and disappointment. In some ways the Israelites in the time of the judges were like the early American settlers of the West, when the only law came at the hands of circuit-riding judges and strong individual lawmen. But the Israelites, instead of contending against primitive Indian tribes, were themselves only tribes, contending against the sophisticated pagan Philistines with their advanced weapons, their fortified cities, and their commercial sea trade. Would they have to live like this forever? Is this the promise God made to Abraham, Isaac, and Jacob?

Samuel arose as a leader when a great debate was going on. Some said God wanted the tribes to stay as a loose confederation. Others said no, God wanted the tribes to centralize, to get an army, a capital city and, most of all, a king. Samuel showed some of his own godly spirit in being able to gain the respect of both sides. His solution, one that seemed to satisfy all, was to go in search of a king, but only one who was clearly anointed by God, the Lord's Chosen One.

The first man Samuel found who met these divine qualifications was a tall, handsome young warrior, Saul, of the tribe of Benjamin. Samuel performed the crowning ceremony, pouring the anointing oil of God on his head. With the hopes of his people on his shoulders, King Saul began to lead. He won some impressive early victories over neighboring nations who were threatening to destroy his people. Somewhere along the way, however, he went into decline. His spiritual decay, represented by distrust and repudiation of prophets of God like Samuel, was accompanied by emotional instability and outbursts of anger, combined with a paranoid fear that people were out to get him. There was a grain of truth in this last part: the people were turning away from King Saul to a young man named David. The tragic case of Saul has received much attention from psychiatrists as a source of study of mental illness.

Eventually Saul was no longer able to lead, and the people looked back to the aging judge Samuel to take over. Samuel approached the unpredictable Saul with these straightforward words.

1 Samuel 13:13, 14 *"You have disobeyed the commandment of the Lord your God. He was planning to make you and your descendants kings of Israel forever, but now your dynasty must end; for the Lord wants a man who will obey him. And he has discovered the man he wants and has already appointed him as king over his people; for you have not obeyed the Lord's commandment."*

Where would Samuel find such a man after God's own heart? God himself led him to search among the sons of Jesse of Bethlehem in the tribe of Judah. As the older seven sons of Jesse paraded before Samuel he thought each in turn was so fine-looking that God must surely mean him to be king. But the Lord said to him:

1 Samuel 16:7 *"I don't make decisions the way you do! Men judge by outward appearance, but I look at a man's thoughts and intentions."*

Finally the youngest son was called in. He was David,

who had been keeping the sheep. He is described as "a fine looking boy, ruddyfaced, and with pleasant eyes." To him God gave his approval: "This is the one; anoint him." A simple ceremony followed:

1 Samuel 16:13 *So David stood there among his brothers, Samuel took the olive oil he had brought and poured it upon David's head; and the Spirit of Jehovah came upon him and gave him great power from that day onward.*

1 Samuel 16:14 At the same time, however, *"the spirit of the Lord had left Saul."* The Israelites were moving from the tradition of judges to the system of kings, but the leadership of the kings, like that of the judges, was based on *charisma,* a gift of leadership directly from God.

Rarely has there been a man with more powerful *charisma* than David. He was gifted with natural leadership, probably to the point of genius. As a young man, someone said that David

1 Samuel 16:18 *was not only a talented harp player, but was handsome, brave, and strong, and had good, solid judgment.*

But the admirer saw an extra quality:

1 Samuel 16:18 *"What's more,"* he added, *"the Lord is with him."*

## Getting the Story in Mind

Mark the following statements *True* or *False.*

_____ 1. *The Israelites were more advanced technically than any of their neighbors.*

_____ 2. *The last judge of Israel, in the time when judges were the main rulers, was Samuel.*

_____ 3. *When Samuel was a judge, many Israelites began to wish for a strong central government.*

_____ 4. *Samuel believed that God had shown him which man to anoint as king of Israel.*

_____ 5. *The first king of Israel was named David.*

_____ 6. *Samuel showed which man was God's choice for king by putting a crown on his head.*

_____ 7. As king, Saul failed utterly from the start.
_____ 8. Saul's son followed him as king.
_____ 9. David was chosen as the next king because he was the most handsome man among his brothers.
_____ 10. Kingly leadership was a gift from God.

## Getting the Meaning in Hand

1  King Saul may have suffered from the mental disease of
_____ a. paranoia, a fear of persecution from others.
_____ b. schizophrenia, a split or disintegrated personality.
_____ c. hallucinations, perception of objects that do not really exist.
_____ d. kleptomania, a neurotic impulse to steal.

2  A person honored as "the Lord's Chosen One"
_____ a. was the elected choice of the people.
_____ b. was anointed by God due to his brilliant leadership ability.
_____ c. was chosen for inner qualities often hidden from most people.
_____ d. was a fraud, a self-proclaimed divine messenger.

3  Already we have seen a number of social forms taken by the biblical peoples. Match the forms in the list at left with the time in biblical history at right.

_____ 1. slavery
_____ 2. military
_____ 3. local autonomy
_____ 4. patriarchy

_____ 5. monarchy
_____ 6. nomadic

a. Abraham, Isaac, and Jacob
b. Egypt under Pharaoh
c. Canaan in the time of Joshua
d. Canaan in the time of the judges
e. Canaan in the time of Saul
f. Israelites led by God in the wilderness

# 15 David's Journey to Power / *1 Samuel 17–31; 2 Samuel 1–10*

Can one man combine the gifts of thought and action? Can a person be a musician as well as a warrior, a poet as well as a politician? What shall we make of a man who can wield ruthless power yet feel tender emotions, achieve both worldly success and spiritual depth?

When we look at the life of David, the most famous king of Israel, we are astounded. Here is a man who can express genuine love for his friends while calculating political advantage. Here is a man who binds a nation together but watches his family fall apart. Self-confident, shrewd, impulsive, penitent—we can say all this and still not exhaust the soul of this man.

David's rise to leadership of his people began with the anointing by Samuel, but he attracted the attention of his countrymen only later, after his victorious duel with Goliath, the Philistine giant. David's popularity increased in spite of Saul's vengeance-filled attempts to murder him. David had

to hide from Saul for years, yet even in hiding he gathered
a small but growing band of loyal followers.

Part of David's popularity was due to his scrupulous honor
in dealing with Saul, in contrast to Saul's own attitude. To
David, Saul's life was sacred because he had been anointed
king at God's command. Twice he had the opportunity to
kill Saul with a single stealthy blow. When a companion
suggested it once, David replied,

1 Samuel  *"Don't kill him, for who can remain innocent after attacking the*
26:9, 10  *Lord's chosen king? Surely God will strike him down some day, or*
*he will die in battle or of old age.*

David kept in contact with the palace in spite of Saul. The
king's son, Jonathan, was David's best friend, a man he
loved, David said, as he loved his own soul. He was deeply
grieved when word came to him that King Saul and his
prince Jonathan had been killed in battle with the
Philistines. Warfare and poetry combined in these lines
composed in memory of Jonathan:

2 Samuel  *How much they were loved, how*
1:23  *wonderful they were–*
*Both Saul and Jonathan!*
*They were together in life and in death.*
*They were swifter than eagles, stronger than lions.*

2 Samuel  *How I weep for you, my brother Jonathan;*
1:26  *How much I loved you!*
*And your love for me was deeper*
*Than the love of women!*

With a vacancy on the throne, David progresses in a series of
diplomatic moves and military victories to assert his right as
the "Lord's chosen." The royal family of Saul, unwilling to
admit that the power had passed to another lineage, tried
to name a successor from among their own. David,
however, secures a pledge of allegiance from the tribe of
Judah, his own tribe, and then of the remaining tribes.
Instead of attacking the palace in Saul's hometown of
Gibeah, David conquers the city of the Jebusite people, a
city known as Jerusalem. Lying between the two regions

where his power was potentially greatest, the city of Jerusalem made an ideal capital. It was also not far from David's little home town of Bethlehem.

The people admired David's devotion to the Lord, illustrated in his decision to bring the ancient Ark of the Covenant to Jerusalem for protection. Established in a newly built palace and secure from his enemies on all sides, David sought to honor the Lord who had so blessed him. He wished to build a temple in which to house the Ark of the Covenant. A prophet of the Lord named Nathan, in whom David learned to confide, revealed to him that he would not be allowed to build the temple. The Lord would, however, set David's son upon his throne, and his son would build the temple. Furthermore, the Lord promised:

2 Samuel  *"Your family shall rule my kingdom forever."*
7:16

Since its conquest about 1000 B.C. by David, the city of Jerusalem has continued to be associated with the "Lord's chosen," the Hebrew word for which is *Messiah*, and the Greek word *Christ*.

## Getting the Story in Mind

Mark the following statements *True* or *False*.

_____ 1. *David was a great warrior and politician, but a man of shallow thoughts.*

_____ 2. *David loved his friends, but was not known for showing mercy to his enemies.*

_____ 3. *As soon as he was anointed, David marched on Saul's palace and took over the country.*

_____ 4. *While Saul was trying to murder David, David passed up the two chances he had to kill Saul.*

_____ 5. *The crown prince, Jonathan, joined his father's attempts to kill David, who was his rival to the throne.*

_____ 6. *David was happy to hear that Saul and Jonathan were dead and could no longer keep him from the throne.*

_____ 7. *David became king first over his own tribe, Judah, and only later over the whole nation.*

_____ 8. *David chose the neutral city of Jerusalem as the political and religious capital of his new kingdom.*

_____ 9. *Through his prophet Nathan, God promised David that one of his descendants would always be the "Lord's anointed."*

_____ 10. *The Hebrew word for "Lord's chosen" is Messiah, and the Greek word is Christ.*

## Getting the Meaning in Hand

Check the phrase that best completes the sentence:

1 *The personality of David demonstrates that*
_____ a. *religion is principally for women and children.*
_____ b. *poetry and music are marks of effeminacy.*
_____ c. *the gifts of thought and action can be combined in the same man.*
_____ d. *religious people tend to be calculating, hypocritical, and neurotic.*

2 *Ideally, political power in Israelite history was*
_____ a. *avoided by God-fearing people.*
_____ b. *desirable as a way to force others to believe in God.*
_____ c. *a heavy responsibility for which all rulers were held accountable.*
_____ d. *the principal goal of religious leaders.*

# 16 David's Journey Inward / *The Psalms*

The secret of David's political successes was the strength he
drew from his inner life of prayer. Such men have been rare
in history, and the private thoughts of men like Abraham
Lincoln and Dag Hammarskjöld reveal a deep spiritual
need unseen by the boisterous public.

The stories of the life of David in the First and Second Books
of Samuel contain examples of his inner prayer life. Even
more impressive are the *Psalms,* a collection of songs and
poems used for centuries in the worship of the people of
God. More than seventy of these psalms are said to have been
written by or for David. No doubt his reign was a period of
great spiritual activity and renewal of faith in God for a
battle-weary, faith-tested people.

Some of the Psalms are the solitary cries of a man in need
of his God. Others are triumphant shouts of praise for a
throng of worshipers. Some exalt the solitary life, away from
city noise, out on the countryside:

Psalm
23:1, 2
*Because the Lord is my Shepherd, I have everything I need! He lets me rest in the meadow grass and leads me beside the quiet streams.*

Other psalms echo the royal majesty and splendor of the palace:

Psalm
24:7-9
*Open up, O ancient gates, and let the King of Glory in. Who is this King of Glory? The Lord, strong and mighty, invincible in battle. Yes, open wide the gates and let the King of Glory in.*

The lonely man, feeling forsaken even by God, nevertheless cries out:

Psalm
22:1-4
*My God, my God, why have you forsaken me? Why do you refuse to help me or even to listen to my groans? Day and night I keep on weeping, crying for your help, but there is no reply—for you are holy.*

God is beyond time and space, the eternal, infinite power of the universe:

Psalm
90:1, 2
*Lord, through all the generations you have been our home! Before the mountains were created, before the earth was formed, you are God without beginning or end.*

Nature itself reveals the evidence of God to the believer:

Psalm
148:7-13
*Praise him down here on earth, you creatures of the ocean depths. Let fire and hail, snow, rain, wind and weather, all obey. Let the mountains and hills, the fruit trees and cedars, the wild animals and cattle, the snakes and birds, the kings and all the people, with their rulers and their judges, young men and maidens, old men and children—all praise the Lord together.*

Not even the rulers in international affairs work outside God's plan:

Psalm
2:1, 3, 4
*What fools the nations are to rage against the Lord! "Come, let us break his chains," they say, "and free ourselves from all this slavery to God." But God in heaven merely laughs.*

But the rulers of God's people have special responsibilities:

Psalm 72:1-4 *O God, help the king to judge as you would, and help his son to walk in godliness. Help him to give justice to your people, even to the poor. May the mountains and hills flourish in prosperity because of his good reign. Help him to defend the poor and needy and to crush their oppressors.*

The law that the Lord gave the people through Moses is worthy of praise:

Psalm 19:7-9 *God's laws are perfect. They protect us, make us wise, and give us joy and light. God's laws are pure, eternal, just.*

Even the history of the Israelites, sins, rebellions and all, makes a worthy subject for a psalm, as number 106 for example, that tells of "the Lord's mighty acts" in contrast to the people who "quickly forgot all he had done."

The psalms of Israel remain an incomparable treasure of spiritual power. The basic emotions of joy and grief, patience and anger, doubt and faith, and the basic concerns of birth, life, death, marriage, vocation, national affairs, knowledge, and religion are laid before God in prayer and praise.

## Getting the Story in Mind

On the left are lines from some of the Psalms quoted in the reading above. On the right, in scrambled order, are descriptions of the mood or setting of the psalms quoted. Match the mood with the scripture by writing the letter by the correct number.

_____ 1. "Because the Lord is my Shepherd, I have everything I need."

_____ 2. "Open up, O ancient gates, and let the King of Glory in."

_____ 3. "My God, my God, why have you forsaken me?"

a. *Suffering near despair*
b. *Prayer for a ruler of God's people*
c. *A pleasant countryside*
d. *Praise of God's law*
e. *Praise of God, the Creator*
f. *Praise of God as King*

———— 4. *"Before the earth was formed, you are God...."*

———— 5. *"Help him to defend the poor and needy...."*

———— 6. *"They protect us, make us wise and give us joy and light."*

## Getting the Meaning in Hand

*Some Thoughts on Prayer.* Check the three phrases that complete each sentence:

1 *In order for prayer to be meaningful, we must believe*

———— *a. that there is a personal, holy God.*

———— *b. that this God is present to him who prays.*

———— *c. that a real fellowship may be established with this God.*

———— *d. that we are deserving of the privilege of prayer.*

2 *The central purpose of prayer is* not

———— *a. to remind God to do something he might otherwise have forgotten.*

———— *b. to ask him to confer a benefit he might otherwise have withheld.*

———— *c. to get help for a problem in an emergency that we might in a normal time have solved for ourselves.*

———— *d. to experience the fellowship between our finite spirit and the infinite Spirit.*

3 *We learn to pray chiefly through*

———— *a. reading the prayers of others.*

———— *b. personal practice.*

———— *c. both devotional readings and personal practice.*

———— *d. waiting to get in the mood.*

# 17 David's Journey Downward / 2 Samuel 11–19

David's stay at the top was cut short one evening when, the Bible says,

2 Samuel 11:2 *"he couldn't get to sleep and went for a stroll on the roof of the palace."*

Out there, the story continues,

*"he noticed a woman of unusual beauty taking her evening bath."*

The details from there on out are familiar to every movie-goer, for it is the kind of lurid story that draws long lines to the box office.

He sent messengers to bring her to the palace. After she went back home, she discovered that she was pregnant.

Her name was Bathsheba. She was the wife of Uriah, one of David's own officers. David, trying to avoid a scandal, sent for Uriah to come in from the battlefield on the pretense of getting a battle report. But Uriah, far more honorable than his kind, refused to sleep in the comfort of his own home while his comrades camped in the field. Even when David held a banquet in Uriah's honor and tried to get him drunk, he kept control of himself.

Still trying to cover his guilt with Bathsheba, David sent Uriah back to the battlefield with his own death warrant:

2 Samuel 11:15   *The letter instructed Joab to put Uriah at the front of the hottest part of the battle—and then pull back and leave him there to die!*

The generals obeyed their king and Uriah and some of his comrades were killed.

When Uriah's widow had finished her period of mourning, David took her into his house and made her his wife, to join a number of other women with that dubious distinction. "But," says the writer of the Second Book of Samuel, "what David had done was wrong in the eyes of the Lord."

Nathan, the prophet, was not long in coming. With a touching parable, he struck David's heart:

2 Samuel 12:1-6   *"There were two men in a certain city, one very rich, owning many flocks of sheep and herds of goats; and the other very poor, owning nothing but a little lamb he had managed to buy. It was his children's pet and he fed it from his own plate and let it drink from his own cup; he cuddled it in his arms like a baby daughter. Recently a guest arrived at the home of the rich man. But instead of killing a lamb from his own flocks for food for the traveler, he took the poor man's lamb and roasted it and served it."*

*David was furious. "I swear by the living God," he vowed, "any man who would do a thing like that should be put to death; he shall repay four lambs to the poor man for the one he stole, and for having no pity."*

The prophet then said to David,
"You are that rich man."

We would do well to pause here to ask an obvious question: why would a man in David's position allow the news of an event like this to get out? And why, of all places, do we read of scandals like this in the Bible, the Word of God? What we know of human nature leads us to expect a cover-up. Modern leaders in business, government and entertainment often hire expensive public relations firms to help them put only their best image in public view. The public is seldom fooled. When the public sees only a smiling, hand-shaking, back-slapping image of a famous figure, we put him down as a phony. In contrast to the cosmetics of the 20th century, it is refreshing to discover the realism of the biblical narratives. The books of Samuel, Kings, and Chronicles tell the story of Israel's leaders from Saul and David down through many generations. The frankness and the honesty of the situations revealed ring true.

The message of the Bible is about a living God acting in history among flesh-and-blood men. The greatness of that message is all the more appreciated in a time when millions have all but forgotten simple honesty.

## Getting the Story in Mind

Mark the following statements *True* or *False*.

_____ 1. *David's reign as king was unstained by moral failure.*

_____ 2. *Since David was king, he deserved to have any woman he wanted.*

_____ 3. *As soon as Bathsheba became pregnant, David publicly admitted that he was the father.*

_____ 4. *David courageously dueled Bathsheba's enraged husband to see who would win her.*

_____ 5. *Bathsheba was the only woman David ever loved.*

_____ 6. *Since Nathan the prophet was a friend and ally of the king, he overlooked David's misdeed.*

_____ 7. *To the king, who had once been a shepherd, Nathan's story was one he could truly understand.*

_____ 8. *The Bible glosses over the faults of David, a "man after God's own heart."*

## Getting the Meaning in Hand

It is easy to condemn David for what he did, but it is also easy to understand how he could have been tempted to do it. A temptation is a test—not of what you know, but of what you believe and what you are. We've seen Abraham tested by the command to sacrifice Isaac. He passed the test. We've seen David tempted by Bathsheba. He failed.

Below are some temptations that test people today. Check the three which come nearest to some that you have had.

_____ 1. *Not long ago you made a hasty promise. Now comes the time to keep it and you really don't want to....*

_____ 2. *You know you shouldn't do it, but everybody else is getting away with it....*

_____ 3. *Somebody has fainted near you on the street. Nobody else tries to help. You'll be late for work if you stop....*

_____ 4. *Your neighbor brags to you about his recent salary raise....*

_____ 5. *Someone repulsive to you sits down next to you in an auditorium.*

_____ 6. *A member of your family has made a change in religious beliefs and now he is trying to change yours, too....*

_____ 7. *A child is begging you to play with him for a few minutes, but after a hard day's work....*

_____ 8. *The one you love tells you, "If you really loved me, you'd...."*

_____ 9. *You promised to go to a community-improvement meeting tonight, but there is a very good movie on TV....*

_____ 10. *You are planning a small party. Most of the guests say they will not come if one of your friends, whom they dislike, is invited....*

_____ 11. *In the mail this morning was a package from a mail-order store containing a beautiful set of expensive luggage. You didn't order it. A close friend advises you to wait for the store to discover its mistake and contact you....*

_____ 12. *In the upcoming local primary election two candidates have equal appeal to you except that one is campaigning for a new recreation center in your community, the other for a new school in a poorer neighborhood farther away....*

# 18 David's Journey Upward / Psalm 51

David is known for his power as a warrior, a ruler, a poet. His greatest characteristic comes not out of his power, however, but out of his weakness. In his weakness, David had the capacity to repent, to start over. Here lies his greatness.

After Nathan, the prophet, had uttered the penetrating words, "You are the man," he predicted a series of calamities to fall on David's family. The child Bathsheba would bear is to die in infancy. Beyond that, Nathan prophesied,

2 Samuel 12:11, 12 *"I vow that because of what you have done I will cause your own household to rebel against you. I will give your wives to another man, and he will go to bed with them in public view. You did it secretly, but I will do this to you openly, in the sight of all Israel."*

We know of some events that occurred in David's troubled

family: a revolution attempted by his son Absalom; a sexual
assault by his son Amnon upon David's daughter Tamar;
the later murder of Amnon; the execution of Absalom.

David's grief over the disintegration of his home life
awakened his soul. He humbled himself before the justifiable
wrath of the God he had loved.

To do things that are clearly wrong, and to fail to do
things that are clearly right, lead to a feeling of guilt. Often
this guilt eats away at a person's peace of mind. It lies buried
deep in a person's thoughts. It is often impossible to admit the
source of guilt. The more one refuses to admit misdeeds,
the harder it becomes to act rightly, which leads to more
guilt, in a downward spiral that ultimately destroys. Only
repentance and confession of wrongs can free a person from
this sense of guilt. When one has the faith that he can cast his
burdens on God, that he can be forgiven and start over
again, then guilt can be removed. As long as a person
thinks of God as a giant computer bank, storing up all his
sins to be used against him in some cosmic congressional
hearing, there can be no salvation, no restoration.

David was able to trust God. He could repent and confess
his wrongs, and start over again in newness of life. He
could talk to God in the words of the great psalm of
repentance, Psalm 51 in our Bibles. He could pray:

Psalm
51:1, 2
*O loving and kind God, have mercy. Have pity upon me and take
away the awful stain of my transgressions. Oh, wash me, cleanse
me from this guilt. Let me be pure again.*

David could confess his sin:

Psalm
51:3, 4
*For I admit my shameful deed–it haunts me day and night. It is
against you and you alone I sinned, and did this terrible thing. You
saw it all, and your sentence against me is just.*

Instead of wringing his hands and dwelling on his sins,
David had the courage to be willing to start over:

Psalm
51:10-12
*Create in me a new, clean heart, O God, filled with clean thoughts
and right desires. Don't toss me aside, banished forever from your
presence. Don't take your Holy Spirit from me. Restore to me*

*again the joy of your salvation, and make me willing to obey
you.*

David also knew that being cleansed from sin would lead to a
new sense of worship and service, not merely lip worship
and boastful service, but a sincere and humble life:

Psalm *You don't want penance; if you did, how gladly I would do it! You*
51:16, 17 *aren't interested in offerings burned before you on the altar. It is a
broken spirit you want—remorse and penitence. A broken and a
contrite heart, O God, you will not ignore.*

The spirit of David—the spirit of faith, of penitence, of
confession, of cleansing—would mark the people of God in
the centuries to come.

## Getting the Story in Mind

Multiple choice. Choose the correct ending for the following
statements or answers for the questions.

1 *Check the seven words that describe David:*
_____ *a. fighter*     _____ *g. Messiah, the*
_____ *b. ruler*            *Lord's*
_____ *c. priest*            *anointed*
_____ *d. poet*      _____ *h. philanderer*
_____ *e. singer*     _____ *i. model parent*
_____ *f. prophet*    _____ *j. penitent*

2 *Which of the following was not punishment David received for his
sin?*
_____ *a. he himself would be struck dead.*
_____ *b. his son would die as a result of his sin.*
_____ *c. his family would experience rebellion and scandal.*

3 *David responded to Nathan's stinging words by*
_____ *a. growing angry and sending the prophet to prison.*
_____ *b. being struck by his own guilt.*
_____ *c. arguing that all men do something wrong once in a while.*
_____ *d. giving up because of his own worthlessness.*

## Getting the Meaning in Hand

The Psalm treated in this lesson traces the journey of the soul as it moves from sin to forgiveness. Match the Scripture quotations on the right to the attitudes they represent.

_____ 1. *prayer to a gracious, loving God*

_____ 2. *desire for cleansing*

_____ 3. *confession of sin*

_____ 4. *courage to start over*

_____ 5. *sincere, humble life*

a. *"Create in me a new, clean heart."*

b. *"Let me be pure again."*

c. *"It is a broken spirit you want—remorse and penitence."*

d. *"I admit my shameful deed."*

e. *"O loving and kind God, have mercy."*

Here are the answers to the questions you have found at the end of each part of this lesson. Scripture references are provided, where appropriate, to direct you to the source of the answers.

## 13 After Moses, a Time of Violence

*GETTING THE STORY IN MIND*
1 False *(Deuteronomy 34:4, 5)*
2 True *(Joshua 7:2)*
3 False *(Joshua 6:1-7)*
4 True *(Joshua 7:10-12)*
5 False *(Judges 19:1)*
6 True *(Joshua 18:1)*
7 False *(Joshua 23:8)*
8 True *(Judges 2:16)*

## 14 The People Demand a Ruler

*GETTING THE STORY IN MIND*
1 False *(1 Samuel 13:19-22)*
2 True *(1 Samuel 7:15; Acts 13:20)*
3 True *(1 Samuel 8:4, 5)*
4 True *(1 Samuel 10:1)*
5 False *(1 Samuel 9:17)*
6 False *(1 Samuel 10:1)*
7 False *(1 Samuel 11:15)*
8 False *(1 Samuel 13:13, 14)*
9 False *(1 Samuel 16:6, 7)*
10 True *(1 Samuel 16:13, 14)*

*GETTING THE MEANING IN HAND*
1 a *(1 Samuel chapters 18-27)*
2 c *(1 Samuel 16:6, 7)*
3 1) b
   2) c
   3) d
   4) a
   5) e
   6) f

## 15 David's Journey to Power

*GETTING THE STORY IN MIND*
1 False *(1 Samuel 16:18)*
2 False *(1 Samuel 24:11)*
3 False *(1 Samuel 16:13; 16:19-21)*
4 True *(1 Samuel 24:11; 26:8, 9)*
5 False *(1 Samuel 20:16, 17)*
6 False *(2 Samuel 1:23-26)*
7 True *(2 Samuel 2:1-4)*
8 True *(2 Samuel 5:6-10)*
9 True *(2 Samuel 7:16)*
10 True *(John 1:41; 4:10; Acts 4:26; 10:38)*

*GETTING THE MEANING IN HAND*
1  c *(1 Samuel 16:18)*
2  c *(1 Samuel 10:24; 1 Samuel 13:13, 14; Psalm 72:1-4)*

# 16 David's Journey Inward

*GETTING THE STORY IN MIND*
1  c *(Psalm 23:1)*
2  f *(Psalm 24:7)*
3  a *(Psalm 22:1)*
4  e *(Psalm 90:2)*
5  b *(Psalm 72:4)*
6  d *(Psalm 19:7)*

*GETTING THE MEANING IN HAND*
1  a, b, c *(Psalm 22)*
2  a, b, c *(Psalm 90)*
3  a, b, c *(Psalm 19)*

# 17 David's Journey Downward

*GETTING THE STORY IN MIND*
1  False *(2 Samuel 11:27)*
2  False *(2 Samuel 12:6)*
3  False *(2 Samuel 11:5-13)*
4  False *(2 Samuel 11:14, 15)*
5  False *(2 Chronicles 11:21)*
6  False *(2 Samuel 12:7)*
7  True *(2 Samuel 12:5, 6)*
8  False *(2 Samuel 11:27)*

# 18 David's Journey Upward

*GETTING THE STORY IN MIND*
1  a,b,d,e,g,h,j
2  a *(2 Samuel 12:11-14)*
3  b *(2 Samuel 12:13)*

*GETTING THE MEANING IN HAND*
1  e *(Psalm 51:1)*
2  b *(Psalm 51:2)*
3  d *(Psalm 51:3)*
4  a *(Psalm 51:10)*
5  c *(Psalm 51:17)*

## CHECK YOUR PROGRESS
If your score on Part Three is:
  0-39   You're still wandering in the wilderness.
  40-49  You've crossed the Jordan into the Promised Land.
  50-59  You've won the Battle of Jericho.
  60-69  You're living in the free-swinging days of the Judges.
  70-79  You're in the more civilized time of King Saul.
  80-88  You're in the palace of David. Congratulations, but be careful.

## Part Four

# JEREMIAH

### A People Opposes God and Is Restored

# 19 Introducing You to the Prophets

The last seventeen books of the Old Testament were all written by or about Israel's prophets. They are arranged in your Bible together as a unit. But the prophets lived at the same time as the kings of Israel—those who followed Saul, David, and Solomon. In fact, a number of prophets are mentioned in the books of 1 and 2 Samuel, 1 and 2 Kings, and 1 and 2 Chronicles. Perhaps no part of the Bible is less known than the prophets. But no part is more powerfully relevant to our lives today.

Through the centuries the books of the prophets have been divided into two groups. The first five, Isaiah, Jeremiah, Lamentations, Ezekiel, and Daniel, are called the "Major Prophets" and the last twelve are called the "Minor Prophets." These labels have nothing to do with their importance; they refer to the size of the books the prophets left us.

The word "prophet" along with the noun "prophecy" and the verb "to prophesy" are probably familiar to you.

Perhaps they convey to you the idea of predicting events in
the future, particularly the great event of the coming of the
Messiah or Savior. The prophets were known in their own
day, however, both for telling the distant future, and also
for declaring the Word of the Lord for the times in which
they lived. *Foretelling* the future act of God in Jesus Christ
and *forthtelling* the present acts of God in history: these were
the dual roles of the prophets.

Prophets in Israel are usually seen in two ways. First, we
can divide them into the *writing* prophets and the
*nonwriting* prophets. Not all the prophets had collections
of their prophecies written down. We've already noticed
Nathan, the prophet who stood up to mighty King David and
told him the truth about his affair with Bathsheba. Then
there were prophets like Elijah and Elisha who were the
conscience of the nation when the kings were corrupt. In
most cases, even the writing prophets first spoke their
prophecies—to kings, to crowds of people, to small groups of
disciples—words which were later written down,
preserved, and treasured through the centuries down to
our own time.

Unfortunately, not all the prophets who spoke to God's
people were *true* prophets. Yes, there were false prophets
then, too (and always have been), claiming to bring the
Word of the Lord. An important difference between the
true and the false was, of course, that what the true
prophets predicted actually came to pass, while the
predictions of the false prophets did not.

How to tell the true messenger of God from the
imposter—that was one of the great problems for the
people of God, as it still is today. It was even harder when
the prophets predicted events centuries away, since it was
impossible to wait to see who was right. In general, though,
we can say that the false prophets uttered what the people
wanted to hear, good things about themselves, promises
of victory in battle, words of comfort and peace. The true
prophets on the other hand, uttered warnings of coming
destruction, painful words about the sinfulness of the people,
and the need to repent. Another difference was that the true
prophets spoke their words out of deep love and concern
for their people, while the false prophets exploited the

people for their own gain. People looking for the easy way out were usually fair game for the false prophet. We'll see something of the clash between true and false prophets later in the lesson.

David the king represented the pinnacle of hopes in the Israelite nation for worldly power, honor, and glory. Between the year 1000 B.C. when David began to reign, and 587 B.C. when his magnificent capital, Jerusalem, fell to the Babylonian invaders, lie four centuries of uneven spiral downward into moral, religious, and political decay. Afterward came seventy years of captivity and over a century of struggle to restore the nation to peace, security, and right worship of God. This was the era of the prophets.

We have already seen that even David's own reign was not immune to moral failure and civil strife. His son Solomon raised the nation to its golden age of wealth. That wealth was used to build a magnificent temple to the Lord, yet that same wealth also led to concessions to the pagan religions, principally to please the thousand wives Solomon had taken as part of his treaties with other nations. By the time Solomon's son, Rehoboam, came to the throne with even bolder schemes for power, ten of the twelve tribes revolted. These ten northern tribes kept the name Israel and built a new capital at Samaria. Only two tribes, known as the kingdom of Judah, remained loyal to Jerusalem. The northern kingdom of Israel lasted 200 years, but in 722 B.C. the people were carried into captivity by Assyria, never to return to Samaria as a powerful people again.

The kingdom of Judah held out 165 years longer, mainly by compromising with whatever nation was in power at the time. Around 600 B.C. the famed King Nebuchadnezzar of Babylon gained power over Palestine. He surrounded Jerusalem, and took the royal family captive, along with 10,000 of Judah's leading nobles, soldiers, and craftsmen. Only the poor, the unskilled, the uneducated, the defenseless were left. When these leftover Judeans rebelled against Nebuchadnezzar, he brought his armies to Jerusalem, laid siege, then destroyed the city, leveling even the majestic temple which Solomon had built.

The true prophets of God foretold the destruction of the

nations. Sadly they cried out their prophecies of doom. Angrily, the people attacked the prophets, imprisoning and even killing them. Tradition says Isaiah was "sawn asunder." Others were expelled from the country.

But the prophets had more than a negative message. They also held out hope of the dawning of a new day. It would not be a day of military victory, but it would be a day of the Lord, a day of his power and love ruling once again, this time in a new, personal way.

There is no more poignant character in biblical history than one of these prophets. His name was Jeremiah. He lived through the critical period when conquerors were surrounding his people's capital city, preparing to starve them out. In the following pages we will see him proclaiming his sad words of doom and his stirring words of hope, his struggles against the false prophets who thought the prophet's warnings of Babylonian takeover smacked of treason; his tragic exile; his ultimate victory.

## Getting the Story in Mind

Mark the following statements *True* or *False*.

_____ 1. *The prophets first arose and ruled in the period following the kings.*

_____ 2. *The books of "major" prophets, as a whole, are longer than the books of the "minor" prophets.*

_____ 3. *Not all the prophets wrote books of prophecy.*

_____ 4. *The prophets were too busy making long-range predictions to concern themselves with problems of their own day.*

_____ 5. *After the death of David's son, Solomon, Israel was blessed with a long period of unity and prosperity.*

_____ 6. *Two tribes revolted and left the other ten tribes.*

_____ 7. *Israel, the northern kingdom, was the first to be conquered by foreign invaders.*

## Getting the Meaning in Hand

Check the phrase that best completes the sentence:

1 *One role the prophets did not have was*

_____ *a. foretelling the future.*

_____ *b. forthtelling the Word of God.*

_____ c. ruling the people.
_____ d. speaking out on contemporary issues.

2 One characteristic of the false prophet was
_____ a. he was easy to detect.
_____ b. he told the people what they wanted to hear.
_____ c. he never claimed to speak the Word of the Lord.
_____ d. he dressed and behaved strangely.

3 One characteristic of the true prophet was
_____ a. it pained him to tell bad news.
_____ b. God always protected him from hardship.
_____ c. he never doubted or felt discouraged.
_____ d. he made predictions that could never be verified.

4 The ultimate message of the prophets was
_____ a. doom and punishment.
_____ b. peace and prosperity.
_____ c. the coming rule of God.
_____ d. military victory.

## Side Trip

To get better acquainted with the prophets, study this chart.

| Prophetic Book (No. of chapters) | Situation Addressed | Message Delivered |
| --- | --- | --- |
| Isaiah (66) | mistreatment of poor, blindness to God | justice and righteousness |
| Jeremiah (52) | faithlessness, unconcern | coming punishment, coming new covenant |
| Lamentations (5) | war, disaster, overthrow of government | grief, mourning, words of comfort |
| Ezekiel (48) | captivity, helplessness, hopelessness | God will overcome |
| Daniel (12) | persecution, suffering | loyalty to God, endurance |

| | | |
|---|---|---|
| *Hosea (14)* | *anarchy, assassination of leaders* | *God's love will not let his people go* |
| *Joel (3)* | *lifeless, mechanical worship and life* | *coming judgments and blessings* |
| *Amos (9)* | *neglect of the poor, reliance on military* | *visions of coming doom and overthrow* |
| *Obadiah (1)* | *siege and captivity* | *divine judgment upon the nations* |
| *Jonah (4)* | *prophet who refuses to speak God's Word to a foreign people* | *the wideness of God's mercy* |
| *Micah (7)* | *religious corruption, moral smugness* | *trust in God, not in self* |
| *Nahum (3)* | *international power struggle* | *God will avenge cruelty and immorality* |
| *Habakkuk (3)* | *God's allowance of evil to prevail* | *the righteous man must live by faith* |
| *Zephaniah (3)* | *imminent foreign invasion* | *only humble repentance will ward off punishment* |
| *Haggai (2)* | *attempt to rebuild the devastated city* | *unity and restoration of spiritual life* |
| *Zechariah (14)* | *the city is restored but wickedness continues* | *coming Prince of Peace, coming Good Shepherd* |
| *Malachi (4)* | *religious leaders mislead the people* | *coming ideal leader* |

# 20 The Tragic Victories of Jeremiah / *Jeremiah 1*

Jeremiah was brought up in a religious home. His father ministered as priest of the Lord at Anathoth, a village near Jerusalem.

As Jeremiah was growing up in the years around 640 B.C., his nation was in an exciting upheaval. Their former overlords, the Assyrians, were too weak to keep Judah from independence any longer. The young King Josiah, who must have been then about the same age as Jeremiah (late teens or early twenties), led this freedom movement himself. As the nation was busy rebuilding and renovating, a great discovery was made. In the temple some workers found a copy of the law of Moses, long lost and ignored. When King Josiah had the laws read to the people, the difference between their own lives and the ideals of God's law was so apparent that the religious reform gained great momentum as it swept across the land.

King Josiah began to tear down the ancient idols and shrines of the fertility gods and sex cults of the

Canaanites. And he tried to uproot the new nature religions with their sun, moon, and star worship imported more recently by the Assyrians. The kingdom of Judah was making its declaration of political and religious independence.

As the reforms got underway, the young king gained a powerful ally. In the thirteenth year of Josiah's reign, reports Jeremiah,

Jeremiah
1:4, 5

*The Lord said to me, "I knew you before you were formed within your mother's womb; before you were born I sanctified you and appointed you as my spokesman to the world."*

Was Jeremiah eager to fulfill this destiny that God had decreed for him? Not at first. Like Moses, he responds first with excuses:

Jeremiah
1:6

*"O Lord God," I said, "I can't do that! I'm far too young! I'm only a youth!"*

Again, as with Moses, the Lord insists that he has chosen the right man. He will not let Jeremiah escape this assignment:

Jeremiah
1:7

*"Don't say that," he replied, "for you will go wherever I send you and speak whatever I tell you to."*

The Lord promises the young man the protection and the power to carry out his mission, telling Jeremiah,

Jeremiah
1:8

*"Don't be afraid of the people, for I, the Lord, will be with you and see you through."*

Jeremiah describes the experience of being called by God in a vivid picture:

Jeremiah
1:9

*Then he touched my mouth and said, "See, I have put my words in your mouth!"*

Then follow the words of his assignment from God:

Jeremiah
1:10

*"Today your work begins, to warn the nations and the kingdoms of the world. In accord with my words spoken through your mouth I*

*will tear down some and destroy them, and plant others and
nurture them and make them strong and great.''*

Every word in this divine commission is important. Before
Judah could be made strong and great again, before she could
be restored to a right relationship with her God, she had to
be torn down and destroyed.

Would the people be willing to heed such a message?
Would they be tempted instead to substitute a less serious
reform instead of a real one? With the answers to these
questions as yet unknown to him, Jeremiah left the small
town of his boyhood for the great capital city.

## Getting the Story in Mind

**Mark the following statements *True* or *False*.**

_____ 1. *Jeremiah was born and raised in a small town.*

_____ 2. *He was still quite young when he became a prophet.*

_____ 3. *A reform was sweeping the country in Jeremiah's youth.*

_____ 4. *Jeremiah opposed the reform.*

_____ 5. *When he heard God's call, Jeremiah immediately accepted.*

_____ 6. *God promised Jeremiah protection.*

_____ 7. *God commissioned Jeremiah to speak only words of comfort.*

## Getting the Meaning in Hand

**Check the phrase that best completes these sentences:**

1 *When they got involved in the reform movement, Jeremiah and
King Josiah were*

_____ *a. experienced, mature leaders.*

_____ *b. young and inexperienced.*

_____ *c. disloyal, outside agitators.*

2 *Jeremiah became a prophet because*

_____ *a. his ancestors had always been prophets.*

_____ *b. he attended a training school for prophets.*

_____ *c. before he was born God planned to call him to prophesy.*

3 *One message Jeremiah was not commissioned with was*

_____ *a. to tear down.*

_____ *b. to nurture.*

_____ *c. to escape.*

_____ *d. to destroy.*

# 21 Jeremiah's First Message for God / Jeremiah 1–5

When Jeremiah arrived in Jerusalem, he had to find a way to reach the people. Not being part of the religious establishment, he was not permitted to speak in the temple. So he began his work in the next best place he could find, just outside the gate of the temple.

As the people streamed to worship one morning, they heard Jeremiah, standing there, crying out his "Thus saith the Lord":

Jeremiah 1:16    *"This is the way I will punish my people for deserting me and for worshiping other gods—yes, idols they themselves have made!"*

"Other gods," "idols they have made." Jeremiah was trying to get them to see their own materialism. Every generation has its own kind of materialism, you see, and prophets down through the centuries have had to be clear and specific. If they had only spoken in generalizations and abstractions, probably none of them would have gotten killed. Jeremiah got specific:

Jeremiah
2:25

*"Why don't you turn from all this weary running after other gods? But you say, 'Don't waste your breath. I've fallen in love with these strangers and I can't stop loving them now!' "*

This was the Canaanite worship he was attacking. It was a belief that sex made the world go 'round. According to Canaanite myths, human life and the life of plants and animals grew whenever the storm god, Baal, had intercourse with his goddess, Ashtoreth. To simulate this action on the part of the gods, Canaanite worship often featured temple prostitution. These were the practices of Canaanite worship the Israelites had taken over into their worship. How starkly these ideas contrasted with the concept of the one God who, without help of man, created and sustained all of the natural world by the power of his Word! But how seductively the Canaanite festivities lured God's people.

The Israelites rejected the First Commandment, "You may worship no other god than me." With this unfaithfulness to God went unfaithfulness to their fellow man, and they broke the other commandments against killing, stealing, adultery, lying, covetousness. The rich and the strong got richer and stronger, while the poor and the weak got poorer and weaker. Jeremiah brought them the Word of the Lord:

Jeremiah
5:26-28

*"Among my people are wicked men who lurk for victims like a hunter hiding in a blind. They set their traps for men. Like a coop full of chickens their homes are full of evil plots. And the result? Now they are great and rich, and well fed and well groomed, and there is no limit to their wicked deeds. They refuse justice to orphans and the rights of the poor."*

Jeremiah warned the people of God's coming punishment:

Jeremiah
5:29

*"Should I sit back and act as though nothing is going on? the Lord God asks. Shouldn't I punish a nation such as this?"*

After these harsh and chilling prophecies of their wickedness and God's punishment, Jeremiah told them that even now the Lord, like a loving father, would take his people back if only they would return:

Jeremiah 4:1, 2    *"O Israel, if you will truly return to me and absolutely discard your idols, and if you will swear by me alone, the living God, and begin to live good, honest, clean lives, then you will be a testimony to the nations of the world and they will come to me and glorify my name."*

How were the people reacting to this message from the Lord? Jeremiah was commanded to find out:

Jeremiah 5:1, 2    *"Run up and down through every street in all Jerusalem; search high and low and see if you can find one fair and honest man! Search every square, and if you find just one, I'll not destroy the city!"*

Jeremiah's report was to the point:

Jeremiah 5:12, 13    *"They have lied and said, 'He won't bother us! No evil will come upon us! There will be neither famine nor war!' God's prophets, they say, 'are windbags full of words with no divine authority. Their claims of doom will fall upon themselves, not us!' "*

How would this God, who is not believed to exist, reveal himself to them? No longer as a lawgiver like Moses, no longer as a king like David, no longer as a prophet like Jeremiah; no, this time in a form far more terrifying and irresistible. He would come in the form of a godless foreign conqueror with fire and sword to punish them, Jeremiah prophesied:

Jeremiah 5:14-16    *"Because of talk like this I'll take your words and prophecies and turn them into raging fire and burn up these people like kindling wood. See, I will bring a distant nation against you, O Israel, says the Lord—a mighty nation, an ancient nation whose language you don't understand. Their weapons are deadly; the men are all mighty."*

Do you think they believed Jeremiah? Would you believe it if someone said that today?

## Getting the Story in Mind

Mark the following statements *True* or *False*.

_____ 1. *Jeremiah courted the favor of religious leaders.*

_____ 2. Jeremiah accused the people of worshiping the work of their own hands.

_____ 3. The people's false religion involved a misunderstanding of the role of sex.

_____ 4. Jeremiah's religious prophecies had nothing to do with social, business, or political issues.

_____ 5. If the people would return to God, all nations would be blessed through them.

_____ 6. Many people denied the existence and power of God.

_____ 7. God would never allow a violent, godless nation to conquer his people.

## Getting the Meaning in Hand

Check the phrase that best completes the sentence:

1 *The term "idolatry" refers to*

_____ a. *ancient stone and wood figurines.*

_____ b. *"things" that people value too highly.*

_____ c. *religions other than one's own.*

2 *The words of the prophecies were not usually*

_____ a. *abstract and general.*

_____ b. *specific, direct, and concrete.*

_____ c. *poetic and powerful.*

3 *The religion of the Canaanites involved the belief that*

_____ a. *sex is the creator and sustainer of God.*

_____ b. *God is the creator and sustainer of sex.*

_____ c. *Sex is meant to be a beautiful and intimate relationship between husband and wife.*

4 *Jeremiah's prophecies indicate that true religion is*

_____ a. *whatever a person sincerely believes.*

_____ b. *a right relationship with God and with others.*

_____ c. *basically a matter of doing good deeds.*

# 22 The Agony and Ecstasy of the Prophet's Life / Jeremiah 7, 15, 20, 28

The effect of King Josiah's reform had been an increase in attendance at worship services. Usually that is an encouraging sign, but in this case Jeremiah was commanded by God to tell them not to make their attendance at worship a substitute for acting justly:

Jeremiah 7:3b-7

*"Even yet, if you quit your evil ways I will let you stay in your own land. But don't be fooled by those who lie to you and say that since the Temple of the Lord is here, God will never let Jerusalem be destroyed. You may remain under these conditions only: If you stop your wicked thoughts and deeds, and are fair to others, and stop exploiting orphans, widows and foreigners. And stop your murdering. And stop worshiping idols as you do now to your hurt. Then, and only then, will I let you stay in this land that I gave to your fathers to keep forever."*

It soon became clear that the people would reject the discipline of God. The man who was bringing the Word of

God to them soon became the target of their wrath and fear.

Jeremiah tried every recourse to get through to the people. We are amazed at his courage as he risks his life to warn them of the danger. They pay no heed.

As Jeremiah predicted, the enemy surrounded the city and waited to starve them out. In desperation Jeremiah paraded through the streets with a wooden ox-yoke on his neck, telling the people to accept the yoke of the conquerors that God was sending upon them. The people accused him of aiding the enemy.

They listened rather to the optimistic words of another prophet:

Jeremiah 28:2, 3
*"The Lord of Hosts, the God of Israel, declares: I have removed the yoke of the king of Babylon from your necks. Within two years I will bring back all the Temple treasures that Nebuchadnezzar carried off to Babylon."*

Jeremiah was suspicious:

Jeremiah 28:8, 9
*"The ancient prophets who preceded you and me spoke against many nations, always warning of war, famine and plague. So a prophet who foretells peace has the burden of proof on him to prove that God has really sent him. Only when his message comes true can it be known that he really is from God."*

The other prophet began a predicting contest with Jeremiah, prophesying peace in their time and light at the end of the tunnel. Jeremiah on the other hand predicted the death of that prophet within the year. Jeremiah won.

Except for David and Moses, we know more about Jeremiah than any other Old Testament figure. He spoke movingly about the currents of his times. He allows us to see into the travail of his own soul, even of his doubts, his complaints to God. We see the pity and the rage which he felt for those who turned away from the Word of the Lord, those who turned in anger to attack Jeremiah himself.

Like the other servants of God through the ages, Jeremiah was a human being. God did not have to turn him into a superman to be able to work through him. We see Jeremiah in weakness as well as in courage. His sufferings and humiliation did not leave his soul unscarred. He could cry out in desperation:

Jeremiah
15:10

*"What sadness is mine, my mother; oh, that I had died at birth. For I am hated everywhere I go."*

He would remember God's call, and he could look at his results and begin to doubt whether he had been tricked:

Jeremiah
20:7

*"O Lord, you deceived me when you promised me your help. I have to give them your messages because you are stronger than I am, but now I am the laughingstock of the city, mocked by all."*

Anyone who has ever tried to serve God becomes discouraged. But in these times of discouragement, there is no place better to turn than these flaming words of Jeremiah:

Jeremiah
20:9

*"I can't quit! For if I say I'll never again mention the Lord—never more speak in his name—then his word in my heart is like fire that burns in my bones, and I can't hold it in any longer."*

He had to speak, regardless of the consequences. Hope in the Lord's deliverance always returned to Jeremiah after these dark nights of the soul, so that he could burst out singing:

Jeremiah
20:13

*"I will sing out in thanks to the Lord! Praise him! For he has delivered me, poor and needy, from my oppressors."*

Chapters 26 through 45 of the Book of Jeremiah contain mainly stories from Jeremiah's life. You've gotten just a taste of them so far. What more rewarding way could you spend an evening than to curl up and follow the adventures of this heroic, yet curious, devoted, yet temperamental, prophet of God!

## Getting the Story in Mind

Mark the following statements *True* or *False*.

_____ 1. *In Jeremiah's time, people were making attendance at worship a substitute for acting justly.*

_____ 2. *Acting justly, according to Jeremiah, meant helping those in need.*

_____ 3. *People accused Jeremiah of aiding the enemy.*

_____ 4. *A false prophet predicted victory and return of captives within two years.*

_____ 5. *The prophets who preceded Jeremiah had always foretold prosperity.*

_____ 6. *Jeremiah once wished he had never been born.*

_____ 7. *Even in times of discouragement, Jeremiah was compelled to speak out.*

## Getting the Meaning in Hand

Check the phrase that best completes the sentence:

1 *True worship for Jeremiah meant*

_____ *a. maintaining fine buildings dedicated to the Lord.*

_____ *b. joining the faith of one's choice.*

_____ *c. communion with God that results in acts of love.*

2 *The best explanation of the people's dislike of Jeremiah is:*

_____ *a. he brought it on himself with his strange behavior.*

_____ *b. the people were simply born wicked and could not change.*

_____ *c. the people found it hard to face unpleasant truth about themselves.*

3 *In his confrontation with the false prophet, Jeremiah*

_____ *a. made long-shot predictions that none of the people could verify.*

_____ *b. promised the people more benefits than his opponent.*

_____ *c. wanted to see which prophet's words came true.*

## Are You a Match for a False Prophet?

Below are ten prophecies from the Bible. Five of them were uttered by false prophets. Can you spot them? Mark the following prophecies *True* or *False.*

_____ 1. *"You'll not die! God knows very well that the instant you eat it you will become like him, for your eyes will be opened—you will be able to distinguish good from evil!"*

_____ 2. *"The entire world will be blessed because of you."*

_____ 3. *"The next seven years will be a period of great prosperity ... but afterwards there will be seven years of famine...."*

———— 4. *"Because of what you have done I will cause your own household to rebel against you."*

———— 5. *"Tell him to go and wash in the Jordan River seven times and he will be healed of every trace of his leprosy."*

———— 6. *"The Lord promises that you will push the Syrians around with these horns until they are destroyed."*

———— 7. *"The Lord of Hosts, the God of Israel, declares: 'I have removed the yoke of the king of Babylon from your necks.' "*

———— 8. *"The day will come, says the Lord, when I will make a new contract with the people of Israel and Judah."*

———— 9. *"Within two years I will bring back all the Temple treasures that Nebuchadnezzar carried off."*

———— 10. *"He'll never come! Why, as far back as anyone can remember everything has remained exactly as it was since the first day of creation."*

# 23 The Prophet of Doom Becomes a Prophet of Hope / Jeremiah 31, 51

You may recall that about 600 B.C. King Nebuchadnezzar of Babylon surrounded Jerusalem and took 10,000 of Judah's leaders into captivity. Jeremiah lived through this destruction which he predicted. He showed himself a true prophet in a sense we described earlier when he chose to stay and suffer with the miserable remnant left in Judah rather than to go to Babylon where he would have been safely protected. He did not content himself to say, "I told you so."

When the Babylonian army destroyed Jerusalem with its mansions, its palace, even its temple burned to ashes, its mighty walls pulled down, Jeremiah turned his wrath upon the new tyrants. He began to condemn this nation which had been the "rod of Jehovah's anger." And he began to predict the restoration of fallen Judah. Both the condemnations and the predictions made him unpopular with both the conquerors and the puppet government they established.

In a letter to the captives in Babylon, Jeremiah writes:

Jeremiah 51:58a
*"The wide walls of Babylon shall be leveled to the ground and her high gates shall be burned...."*

Jeremiah 51:24
*"Before your eyes I will repay Babylon and all the Chaldeans for all the evil they have done to my people, says the Lord."*

He instructed the messenger who carried the letter to the captives:

Jeremiah 51:63, 64
*"Then, when you have finished reading the scroll, tie a rock to it and throw it into the Euphrates River, and say, 'So shall Babylon sink, never more to rise, because of the evil I am bringing upon her.' "*

Jeremiah shared the sorrow that his people felt over their ruined city. No enemy of his country could have written this elegy:

Jeremiah 31:15
*"In Ramah there is bitter weeping, Rachel is weeping for her children and she cannot be comforted, for they are gone."*

But he comforted them with words of hope:

Jeremiah 31:16, 17
*"Don't cry any longer, for I have heard your prayers and you will see them again; they will come back to you from the distant land of the enemy. There is hope for your future, says the Lord, and your children will come again to their own land."*

Jeremiah himself eventually was deported to Egypt by the puppet government in Judah. They were not even able to silence him there, for we have more prophecies from him in Egypt.

Of all the powerful and moving prophecies of God coming to us from the lips and pen of Jeremiah, there is one that stands out above all the rest. There is one prophecy that looks back over the history of God's dealings with his people, that looks back to that day when Moses went up on the mountain and brought down the covenant with the Lord. This one great prophecy takes account of the glorious victories of David and the great reforms of King Josiah. He surveys all the history of God's people and sees that it has been a history of God's faithfulness to the covenant and his people's unfaithfulness, of God's patience and man's fickleness:

Jeremiah 31:31, 32     *"The day will come, says the Lord, when I will make a new contract with the people of Israel and Judah. It won't be like the one I made with their fathers when I took them by the hand to bring them out of the land of Egypt—a contract they broke, forcing me to reject them, says the Lord."*

God is preparing something new for his people. He is preparing a new covenant. It will not be a set of laws like the old covenant, a covenant that is easily broken because of the fickleness and weak willpower of the people. What kind of covenant will it be?

Jeremiah 31:33     *"This is the new contract I will make with them: I will inscribe my laws upon their hearts, so that they shall want to honor me; then they shall truly be my people and I will be their God."*

To come to know more about the new covenant, the spiritual bond between the very heart of God and the heart of man, the people of God would have to wait for several agonizing centuries.

## Getting the Story in Mind

Mark the following statements *True* or *False*.

_____ 1. When the nation fell as Jeremiah predicted, his attitude was "I told you so."

_____ 2. Jeremiah had no unkind words for the Babylonians, whom he considered "the rod of Jehovah's anger."

_____ 3. Once Jeremiah instructed that his prophecy be thrown into the river.

_____ 4. As soon as his prediction of destruction came true, Jeremiah shared the sorrow of his people.

_____ 5. Some of Jeremiah's prophecies were hopeful and optimistic.

## Getting the Meaning in Hand

Can you tell the New Covenant from the Old? Based on your

understanding of Jeremiah's prophecy of the New Covenant, mark the following phrases "new" or "old."

_____ 1. *written on stone*

_____ 2. *written on the heart*

_____ 3. *easily broken*

_____ 4. *easily followed*

_____ 5. *based on the willpower of the people*

_____ 6. *based on the forgiving love of God*

# 24 After Jeremiah, The Deluge

During the Babylonian captivity, the people had no king, no priests, no temple, no capital city, no land, no freedom from bondage. Everything the people had trusted in since the days of Abraham seemed to be dashed forever. It was the time of the great crisis for the faith of Israel. What was left for the people to believe in?

Jeremiah had tried to tell them God was justly, though temporarily, punishing his people for continually breaking their side of the covenant. When they had been humbled and brought back to God, he would bring them back to their land. Then would come a "new covenant" with them, written not on tablets of stone, but on their hearts.

As Jeremiah had predicted, some of the exiles were permitted to return to Jerusalem seventy years after its destruction. They were permitted to rebuild the temple and the city walls.

As in the days of Josiah, when the law of God had once before been lost and then recovered, the people set themselves to restoring obedience to the law again. The sacred writings had been handed down separately for generations and had survived the destruction of Jerusalem and the Exile. These inspired writings were collected by scribes into the form that we know today as the books of the Old Testament.

It was a time of hope and new enthusiasm as a group of scribes and doctors of the law, devout men like Ezra and Nehemiah, read the law of God again for the people, explaining it so clearly, they hoped, that the majority of the people might never again stray into idolatry. They dreamed of a people as faithful as Abraham, as obedient as Moses, as mighty as David, as courageous as Jeremiah. Still the former glory never quite returned.

The faith of this new nation of Jews would be tested again and again as they suffered persecution in their own land and were scattered to other lands. A great concern about the suffering of the innocent arose in these times. The need to remain firm and faithful to the one true God even while enduring suffering is the theme of the books of *Job, Ecclesiastes,* and *Daniel,* sacred books that have brought comfort and encouragement to untold millions through the centuries.

The God-fearing people of Judah saw empire strive to overcome empire on their soil. First it was Alexander the Great who overran the land, then the two enemy states into which his empire was divided. Then came the Romans. With every invasion came slaughter, persecution, and oppression. The people could see very little in their present lives that lived up to the glory which God promised his people. They had almost nothing left to cling to but hope and dreams. They read and reread their Scriptures searching to find out how God would reveal himself personally in history, once and for all.

## Getting the Story in Mind

Mark each statement *True* or *False.*

_____ 1. *For about seventy years, the people of God were in captivity.*

_____ 2. *The people lost nearly everything that they had associated with faith in God.*

_____ 3. One thing they never lost, however, was the story of how God had dealt with their ancestors.

_____ 4. This story came to form the Old Testament in our Bibles.

_____ 5. Some of the people were allowed to return and rebuild their city.

_____ 6. This time the people were able to live a life of ease.

_____ 7. Men known as scribes and doctors of the law began to preserve and expound the Scriptures.

_____ 8. Why godly people suffer was not a real problem to the Jews.

_____ 9. The Jews searched the Scriptures to see how God had promised to establish his rule anew.

Put the following words in their appropriate blanks below.

Hint: If you have trouble with these word lists, refer to the Contents of your Bible. If you still have trouble identifying certain books of the Bible, turn to them and browse through them until you can get some idea of their contents. Often the first two or three verses are sufficient.

*Man, Abraham, Isaac, Jacob, Moses, Egypt, desert, Genesis, Exodus, Leviticus, Numbers, Deuteronomy*

A   *The five books of the law open with the _____ or beginnings of God's people: the creation of _____ ; promises to _____ , _____ , and _____ ; the years of slavery in _____ ; the _____ from bondage, their wanderings in the _____ to the death of their great leader _____ . The books of _____ , _____ , and _____ spell out the details of the Law, and recount events from the wanderings.*

*Esther, Ezra, Joshua, Nehemiah, Ruth, Samuel, kings, judges, Chronicles*

B   *The twelve books of history continue the story from the conquest of the promised land under their military leader _____ , the early life in the land under the loose system of _____ , until the godly man _____ anointed the first two ruling _____ . After the* •
*decline and fall of the divided kingdoms, we have the story of the restoration under the scribe _____ and the builder*

_____ . *The two books of* _____ *and*
_____ *are named after heroines whose stories are*
*told. The* _____ *are another version of the history of*
*Israel.*

*Proverbs, Ecclesiastes, Psalms, Song of Solomon, Job*

C  *The five books of poetry tell us of the spiritual and ethical life of the*
*people. How an innocent man endured suffering is the theme of*
_____ . *The "hymnbook" of Israel is the book of*
_____ *while the book of* _____ *is their*
*"almanac" of proverbial wisdom. Two books of the joys and*
*sorrows of human love and life are* _____ *and*
_____ .

*Hosea, Joel, Zephaniah, Isaiah, Amos, Obadiah, Jeremiah, Jonah,*
*Micah, Lamentations, Nahum, Habakkuk, Ezekiel, Haggai,*
*Daniel, Zechariah, Malachi*

D  *The seventeen books of prophecy begin in our Bibles with the major*
*books of prophecy* _____ , _____ ,
_____ , _____ , *and*
_____ . *The twelve minor prophets are*

_____ , _____ , _____ ,
_____ , _____ , _____ ,
_____ , _____ , _____ ,
_____ , _____ , *and*
_____ .

## Getting the Meaning in Hand

Life is like a maze—it's easy to fall into confusion and trouble,
hard to keep plunging ahead. As long as you have
confidence that the path is leading somewhere, it's much
easier to keep going. START in the Garden of Eden, and
follow the people of God until you END with the coming
Messiah.

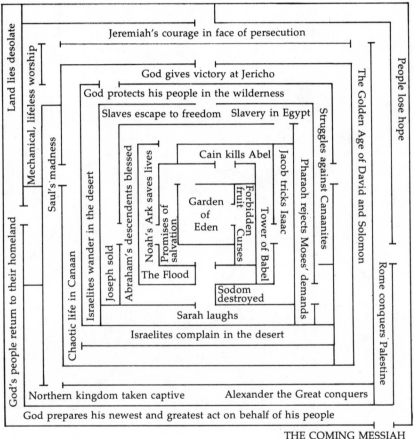

Land lies desolate

Jeremiah's courage in face of persecution

Mechanical, lifeless worship

God gives victory at Jericho

God protects his people in the wilderness

Saul's madness

Slaves escape to freedom   Slavery in Egypt

Struggles against Canaanites

The Golden Age of David and Solomon

People lose hope

Israelites wander in the desert

Abraham's descendents blessed

Noah's Ark saves lives

Cain kills Abel

Jacob tricks Isaac

Pharaoh rejects Moses' demands

God's people return to their homeland

Chaotic life in Canaan

Joseph sold

Promises of salvation

Forbidden fruit

Garden of Eden

Curses

Tower of Babel

The Flood

Sodom destroyed

Sarah laughs

Israelites complain in the desert

Rome conquers Palestine

Northern kingdom taken captive       Alexander the Great conquers

God prepares his newest and greatest act on behalf of his people

THE COMING MESSIAH

Here are the answers to the questions you have found at the end of each part of
this lesson. Scripture references are provided, where appropriate, to direct
you to the source of the answers.

## 19 Introducing You to the Prophets

*GETTING THE STORY IN MIND*
1 False
2 True
3 True
4 False
5 False
6 False
7 True

*GETTING THE MEANING IN HAND*
1 c
2 b
3 a
4 c

## 20 The Tragic Victories of Jeremiah

*GETTING THE STORY IN MIND*
1 True *(Jeremiah 1:1)*
2 True *(Jeremiah 1:6)*
3 True *(2 Chronicles 34:3-7; 2 Kings 22, 23; Jeremiah 1:2)*
4 False *(Jeremiah 11:1-8)*
5 False *(Jeremiah 1:6)*
6 True *(Jeremiah 1:8; Jeremiah 1:18)*
7 False *(Jeremiah 1:9, 10)*

*GETTING THE MEANING IN HAND*
1 b *(Jeremiah 1:6; 2 Chronicles 34:3-7)*
2 c *(Jeremiah 1:4, 5)*
3 c *(Jeremiah 1:10)*

## 21 Jeremiah's First Message for God

*GETTING THE STORY IN MIND*
1 False *(Jeremiah 6:13, 14; Jeremiah 5:31)*
2 True *(Jeremiah 1:16)*
3 True *(Jeremiah 3:1; Jeremiah 2:20)*
4 False *(Jeremiah 5:25-29)*
5 True *(Jeremiah 4:1, 2)*
6 True *(Jeremiah 5:12)*
7 False *(Jeremiah 5:15-17)*

*GETTING THE MEANING IN HAND*
1 b *(Jeremiah 2:27; Jeremiah 1:16)*
2 a *(The vivid pictures the words of the prophets bring to mind are well illustrated in
Jeremiah chapter 2. In that one passage you can find 100 word pictures.)*

3  a *(Jeremiah 2:1; 2:32-35)*
4  b *(Jeremiah 2:13)*

# 22 The Agony and Ecstasy of the Prophet's Life

*GETTING THE STORY IN MIND*
1  True *(Jeremiah 7:1-15)*
2  True *(Jeremiah 7:5, 6)*
3  True *(Jeremiah 38:4; See 38:1-6)*
4  True *(Jeremiah 28:1-4)*
5  False *(Jeremiah 28:8; See 28:5-8)*
6  False *(Jeremiah 15:10) Since "false" is not clear, "true" is also acceptable.*
7  True *(Jeremiah 20:9)*

*GETTING THE MEANING IN HAND*
1  c *(Jeremiah 7:4-7)*
2  c *The false prophet (Jeremiah 28) also acted out strange parables [see sheet].*
3  c *(Jeremiah 28:9-17)*

*TRUE AND FALSE PROPHETS*

|     |       | *Prophecy* | *Result* |
|-----|-------|------------|----------|
| 1.  | False | *Genesis 3:1-5* | *Genesis 3:6-24* |
| 2.  | True  | *Genesis 12:1-3* | *the whole Bible story could be considered the fulfillment of this prophecy.* |
| 3.  | True  | *Genesis 41:29, 30* | *Genesis 41:53-55* |
| 4.  | True  | *2 Samuel 12:13, 14* | *2 Samuel 12:15-20* |
| 5.  | True  | *2 Kings 5:1-10* | *2 Kings 5:11-14* |
| 6.  | False | *1 Kings 22:10-12* | *1 Kings 22:19-23; 34-38* |
| 7.  | False | *Jeremiah 28:2* | *Jeremiah 28:12-14; Jeremiah 52:1-16* |
| 8.  | True  | *Jeremiah 31:31* | *Matthew 26:27-29; Hebrews 8:6, 8* |
| 9.  | False | *Jeremiah 28:3* | *Jeremiah 52:17-23* |
| 10. | False | *2 Peter 3:4* | *2 Peter 3:8-10* |

# 23 The Prophet of Doom Becomes a Prophet of Hope

*GETTING THE STORY IN MIND*
1  False *(Jeremiah 31:15)*
2  False *(Jeremiah 51:24, 58; See 50; 51:1-58)*
3  True *(Jeremiah 51:63, 64)*
4  True *(Jeremiah 31:15; Jeremiah 40:6; 40:1-6)*
5  True *(Jeremiah 31:16-33; See Jeremiah 29-33)*

*GETTING THE MEANING IN HAND*
1  Old *(Exodus 24:12)*
2  New *(Jeremiah 31:33)*
3  Old *(Jeremiah 31:32)*

4  New *(Jeremiah 31:34)*
5  Old *(Exodus 24:7; Exodus 32:1)*
6  New *(Jeremiah 31:34)*

## 24  After Jeremiah, The Deluge

*GETTING THE STORY IN MIND*

1  True
2  True
3  True
4  True
5  True
6  False
7  True
8  False
9  True

A  1. Genesis 2. man 3. Abraham 4. Isaac 5. Jacob 6. Egypt 7. Exodus 8. desert
   9. Moses 10. Leviticus 11. Numbers 12. Deuteronomy
B  1. Joshua 2. judges 3. Samuel 4. kings 5. Ezra 6. Nehemiah 7. Esther 8. Ruth
   9. Chronicles
C  1. Job 2. Psalms 3. Proverbs 4. Ecclesiastes 5. Song of Solomon
D  1. Isaiah 2. Jeremiah 3. Lamentations 4. Ezekiel 5. Daniel 6. Hosea 7. Joel
   8. Amos 9. Obadiah 10. Jonah 11. Micah 12. Nahum 13. Habakkuk
   14. Zephaniah 15. Haggai 16. Zechariah 17. Malachi

## *YOUR ASSESSMENT OF THE PROPHETS*

Now that you are at the halfway point of your journey, your assessment of the
prophets may give a hint of what lies ahead:

| | |
|---|---|
| 50 or under | You have the interest and the patience to continue to the end in spite of difficulty. |
| 51-70 | You have interest and patience—and knowledge to keep you moving ahead. |
| 71-90 | In addition to interest, patience and knowledge, you display a genuine concern to probe below the surface of things. This concern will make the rest of your venture full of surprises and rewards. |
| 91-110 | Along with these other qualities listed above, you have an inner motivation that goes far beyond quizzes and games. |
| 111-131 | In life as well as in study, you can do without carrot-and-stick, reward-and-punishment motivation. Neither money nor praise from others counts as much for you as the quality of what you do. |

# Part Five

# JESUS

## God Sends His Son
## into the World

# 25 The Old Way Ends, The New Way Begins

If you put your finger in your Bible at the place where the Old Testament ends and the New Testament begins, you will see that you are more than three-quarters of the way through the pages. Thousands of years of the history of God's dealings with men have been covered, and only about a hundred years of Bible history remain. In many ways it is the most important century of all, so important that the second half of this Bible course is devoted to it. It is the century of Jesus Christ, his life, death, and resurrection; it is the century that begins the Christian era, the birth of the church and the offer of God's free gift of eternal life to all.

The New Testament books do not simply take up where the last books of the Old Testament leave off. There is a gap of several centuries. So many changes are made that at first glance the situation we find when we read the New Testament seems to bear almost no resemblance to the Old. We find no kings or prophets, no "Hebrews," no "Israelites." The old enemies, Philistines, Assyrians,

Babylonians, are long since gone. Many of the people no longer speak the old Hebrew or Aramaic languages, and the New Testament itself is written in Greek, for that is what most people speak now. All kinds of new religious groups have developed since the close of the Old Testament: the Pharisees and the Sadducees for example, along with Zealots, Essenes, and Hellenists. The biblical people are now called "Jews" and they are no longer concentrated in Palestine, but are scattered all over, with strongholds as far north as Rome and as far south as Alexandria, Egypt.

Some of the topics of religious conversation are new, or at least emphasized far more than in the Old Testament: baptism, the resurrection of the dead, the end of the world, for example, as well as the feeling among many that the time of the coming of a Messiah is near.

The truth is that during these centuries "between the Testaments" the initiative in the tides of history had moved north. No longer were Egypt, Assyria, Babylon, Persia the big powers. The Golden Age of Greece produced great philosophy, art, and political democracy. The great questioner Socrates passed on his wisdom to his brilliant pupil Plato, who in turn was the teacher of Aristotle, who tutored Alexander the Great.

As Greek culture swept across the civilized world through Alexander's military conquests, the Jews were challenged by this new, sophisticated way of life. Some, like the Essenes, reacted by taking to the desert near the Dead Sea to escape all the new ideas. Others, known as "Hellenists" gave in completely, adopting Greek names and clothing styles, Greek schooling and vocations. The most thoughtful, however, tried to come to terms with their changing situations. Some Jews like Philo of Alexandria commended the way of the one God of the Bible in philosophical books aimed at the Greek intellectuals. Others set up schools along Greek lines to teach the Law of Moses and rhetoric. These "synagogue schools," as they were called, were pioneer Bible classes or schools. Most important of all, they translated the Hebrew Scriptures into a Greek version called the Septuagint, and used it to teach Greek-speaking Jews, and to attract converts and sympathizers all over the civilized world.

The rise and decline of Greece changed the course of history. The Greek language spread throughout the known world. People of all backgrounds came in contact with each other. Because of the Greek culture, the way was being prepared for a new faith to arise, a faith that would go into all the world.

## Getting the Story in Mind

Mark the following statements *True* or *False:*

_____ 1. *The Old Testament in your Bible has more than three times as many pages as the New Testament.*

_____ 2. *The Old Testament spans over a thousand years of history of God's dealings with his chosen people.*

_____ 3. *The New Testament covers about one hundred years of Bible history.*

_____ 4. *The New Testament books take up the story of God's people in the years immediately following the Old Testament.*

_____ 5. *The New Testament was written in the Greek language.*

_____ 6. *As the New Testament story begins, most of the Jews have returned to Palestine.*

_____ 7. *Most Jews tried not to have anything to do with the Greek culture.*

_____ 8. *The Septuagint was a translation of the Hebrew scriptures into the Greek language.*

## Getting the Meaning in Hand

*Coping with Change*

Multiple Choice: Check the correct ending to the following sentences:

1 *The Jewish group who formed a religious community near the Dead Sea was trying to*

_____ a. *fight the foreign conqueror.*

_____ b. *compromise with the Greeks.*

_____ c. *withdraw from foreign influences.*

2 *The Hellenists, who left behind their Jewish traditions and adopted Greek ways,*

_____ a. *withdrew from the challenge of change.*

_____ b. *compromised with the Greeks.*

_____ c. *fought the new influence.*

3 *Those who translated the Hebrew scriptures into Greek, and who communicated with the Greek-speaking people,*

_____ *a. tried to escape the new culture.*

_____ *b. compromised with the Greeks.*

_____ *c. tried to cope with the new challenges.*

## *Side Trip*

What are some of the changes in today's world that you have the hardest time dealing with? What is your usual response to these problems? To fight? To compromise? To try to cope? How would you cope with the following changes in your life:

1 *Growing older.*

2 *The changing moral climate.*

3 *Changes in the makeup in your neighborhood.*

4 *Seeing your children grow up.*

5 *More free time.*

6 *More noise, pollution, crowded conditions around you.*

7 *The availability of more new appliances and luxuries.*

# 26 People in Search of Salvation

There was a time, after the glory of Greece began to fade, when the Jews took advantage of a power vacuum to seize control of their own destiny. A family of patriots, the Hashmons, led an army to reclaim their homeland, and the people's hopes began to soar for a new era of God's kingdom on earth. The story of the battles as well as the hopes for better days are available to us in the books of the *Apocrypha*, writings from the period following the close of the Old Testament, revered but not considered as Scripture by the Jews. The Apocrypha appears in some versions of the Bible today. It is worth reading because of its interest and value in leading up to the time of Christ.

Independence and freedom died an early death, however. Quarrels and power struggles broke out periodically between the Sadducees and the Pharisees. The Sadducees were the conservative ruling class, who traced their ancestry back to the tribe of Levi, the priestly tribe of which Moses had been a member. These wealthy

landowners loved stability even if it meant compromising
with whichever neighboring nation was trying to control
them. The Sadducees accepted only the first five books of the
Bible as Scripture, considering the prophets and other
writings as mere interpretations of the Law of Moses.

Against the aristocratic Sadducees were pitted the
Pharisees, more progressive (at least in their early days),
more democratic, and more patriotic. To the Pharisees, the
Law of Moses was a kind of charter or constitution that had
to be continually updated to meet changing situations.
They considered the prophets as the first reinterpreters of
the Law, and their own interpretations and traditions as
continuing the spirit of the prophets. These interpretations
eventually became a mass of legal rules covering all kinds of
situations. Tragically, the important ideals of justice,
mercy, and faith were mixed in and confused with minor
details and petty disputes, leading to a disrespect for the law.

In addition to these large parties, the Jews had their
minority groups. The Essenes, who believed in strict
separation from the secular world, retreated to such
remote places as the caves in the wilderness near the Dead
Sea. Records of one such group were found in 1947 in the
famous Dead Sea Scrolls, the ancient collection of writings
found in caves after being lost for 2,000 years. These groups
spent their lives performing daily baptisms and sharing
religious meals as well as study and commentary on
Scripture. At the opposite pole were groups like the Zealots
who, far from retreating from the world, engaged in guerrilla
warfare and revolutionary attempts to overthrow the
oppressors.

It is often true that when a people is unable or unwilling
to govern themselves, it becomes necessary for an outside
force to step in and do it for them. In the case of the Jews, split
into so many warring factions, it was Rome who stepped
in: the great Empire, beginning as a little city-state, had
spread through many of the lands bordering the
Mediterranean Sea. The power of Rome had grown through a
superior system of roads, building techniques, law
enforcement, and governmental organization. The Greek
language and culture lingered. But it was Rome who took
advantage of any small country's weakness and inner

turmoil. It was Rome who would move into weaker, smaller countries and put into power men who would advance the interests of the Empire, at the expense of local wishes. Jerusalem fell under the heel of Rome after 63 B.C. Rome ruled Jerusalem through puppet kings such as Herod the Great or administrators like Pontius Pilate, both infamous names in the New Testament.

With the end of freedom came a new look to the glorious past, with a longing for a better future. In spite of all their differences, the various groups were agreed on some basic ideals. As they looked to the past, they knew that they were united on two fundamentals: *the Word of God* and the *People of God*. Yet they disputed over what form the Word takes, whether law, or prophecy, or tradition. And they disputed over what form the People would take: whether a nation, a priesthood, a holy community, or a divinely led army. But there was a Word of God. And there was a People of God. On that every believer took his stand.

As they looked to the future, they looked for a prophet like Moses. Had not Moses himself promised:

Deuteronomy 18:15    *"He will raise up for you a Prophet like me, an Israeli, a man to whom you must listen and whom you must obey."*

Many also looked for a priest who would bring the true worship of God, the worship based on a new covenant between God and man, one written on the heart, as Jeremiah had prophesied. Besides the new prophet and the new priest, they looked for a new king and kingdom, one like David of the seed of Jesse, who would bring victory to God's people.

While many longed for a new prophet, priest, or king, it occurred to virtually no one that God would choose to send them all three in one man.

## Getting the Story in Mind

Mark the following statements *True* or *False*.

_____ 1. *The group of books called the Apocrypha contains information about the times following the close of the Old Testament.*

_____ 2. *The Hashmons were foreign invaders who conquered the Jews.*

_____ 3. *The priestly Sadducees accepted only the first five books of the Bible as Scripture.*

_____ 4. *The Pharisees considered further interpretations of Law unnecessary for meeting new situations.*

_____ 5. *The Essenes sought to escape the everyday world by forming small religious communities in the desert.*

_____ 6. *The Zealots attempted to overthrow foreign rule by violent means.*

_____ 7. *The Greeks conquered Palestine in 63 B.C.*

_____ 8. *Most of the Jews stressed two fundamentals: the Word of God and the People of God.*

_____ 9. *The various factions among the Jews all looked for one man to come as prophet, priest, and king.*

_____ 10. *The Apocrypha was respected and read, but not considered Scripture by the Jews.*

# 27 Why God Sent Jesus: For Feeding and Healing

Try to imagine that you are an ordinary citizen of Palestine twenty centuries ago. Faced with all the religious and political confusion, you listen and wonder at the discussions about the Messiah who is to come. You of course have some convictions of your own about it all. Now suppose you had met a follower of Jesus, heard his claims and his testimony. Would you believe him?

Before you answer, think about this: as a 20th century man or woman perhaps you still haven't heard the original teachings of Jesus. Through the centuries a lot of ideas have ridden the coattails of Christianity, and ways of life that are foreign to the message of Jesus claim to be the genuine article. Each time you approach this most important figure ever to walk the earth, you should do so as if it were the first time, with a sense of openness and expectancy.

One of the most revealing pictures of Jesus found anywhere is the story of his temptation in the wilderness by the devil. As told in the Gospel According to Matthew, this experience shows us a great deal about who Jesus was, how he viewed himself, and what he thought about the role of a Messiah. Why did God send Jesus? Much of the answer to this question of the ages stems from a brief but profound narrative at the beginning of Matthew chapter 4. We will take a lingering look at Jesus in this dramatic setting.

We read that very early in his ministry Jesus was led by the Spirit into the desert to be tempted by Satan (Matthew 4:1). Forty days and nights he did without food. He had begun to feel the sharp pains and dull weakness of hunger when he found himself face to face with this challenge:

**Matthew 4:3** *Satan tempted him to get food by changing stones into loaves of bread.*
*"It will prove you are the Son of God," he said.*

What could be wrong with that? Shouldn't a hungry man use the means at his disposal to get food? If Jesus had the power to turn stones into bread, why not use that power?

There was more to the Tempter's suggestion than eating: *"prove* you are the son of God...." Jesus' credentials were being challenged. Jesus recognized further that this temptation was not merely to feed himself one time. It was a temptation to choose economic power as the way to bring God's will to men. Jesus sensed the seriousness of this temptation, so his answer was not to the smaller question of turning stones into bread, but to the larger question of bread as the means to power:

**Matthew 4:4** *Jesus told him, "No! For the Scriptures tell us that bread won't feed men's souls: obedience to every word of God is what we need."*

It was a truth that Jesus demonstrated by going forty days without food. But it was a truth that well-fed, overweight, affluent people could never quite grasp. The poor and needy, of course, knew this lesson well. For them Jesus had great compassion. "Not by bread alone" was not the same thing as "not by bread at all." Jesus did not intend to ignore physical needs. Indeed, he is known as the "Great Physician," healing the lame, the leper, the blind, the demon-possessed, those troubled in countless other ways. Once he fed five thousand people, another time four thousand. He knew that bread was necessary for life, but he taught his followers to rely on God alone for life and bread.

Jesus knew that even when a man's physical needs are assured, a far greater need, a spiritual need, remains to be filled. His kingdom, unlike the empires of the Egyptians, Assyrians, Greeks, Romans, unlike even the kingdom of Israel under David, would concentrate on the spiritual need. He knew that if people were enabled to live free from guilt and full of compassion, they could solve their physical needs. But without spiritual power, every economic plan would end in bureaucracy, corruption, futility.

## Getting the Story in Mind

Mark the following statements *True* or *False*.

_____ 1. *Because Jesus was God's Son, he was never tempted to do wrong like ordinary people.*

_____ 2. *The Spirit urged Jesus to avoid confrontation with Satan.*

_____ 3. *The Spirit led Jesus into the wilderness to be tempted by the devil.*

_____ 4. *Jesus did not change the stones into bread because he was not hungry at the time.*

_____ 5. *Jesus never concerned himself with the physical needs of people.*

_____ 6. *Jesus knew there was a spiritual hunger in men deeper even than hunger for bread.*

_____ 7. *Jesus answered the devil with words from Scripture.*

## Getting the Meaning in Hand

Choose *two* of the following ideas about food, often heard today, that are most nearly in harmony with Jesus' words, "Man cannot live by bread alone."

_____ 1. *Feeding hungry people is not as important as going to church regularly.*

_____ 2. *Going to church regularly is not as important as feeding hungry people.*

_____ 3. *People need to feed their souls as well as their stomachs.*

_____ 4. *Starvation is actually necessary to keep the world's population in control.*

_____ 5. *Religion is a luxury that keeps people's minds off of the basic necessities—food, clothing, and shelter.*

_____ 6. *Love of God and concern for the hungry go hand in hand.*

_____ 7. *If anyone goes hungry today, it's his own fault.*

## Side Trip

This lesson pointed to Jesus' many miracles of compassion for people. You can read about some of them in the following passages:

1 *A soldier's son is cured of paralysis by "remote control." Matthew 8:5-13*

2 *Healing a man leads some to plot to kill Jesus. Matthew 9:8-14*

3 *A possessed man, living among tombs, is cured by Jesus. Mark 5:1-20*

4 *Jesus feeds 5,000 people with a small lunch. Mark 6:30-44*

5 *Jesus heals an epileptic boy. Mark 9:14-29*

6 *Jesus heals a hunch-backed woman and is criticized for it. Luke 13:10-17*

7 *A blind beggar receives his sight. Mark 10:46-52*

8 *Jesus heals one of the men in the mob trying to arrest him. Luke 22:47-53*

# 28 Why God Sent Jesus: For Signs and Wonders

No sooner had Jesus resisted the Tempter's first suggestion, when he was faced with another:

Matthew
4:5

*Satan took him to Jerusalem to the roof of the Temple.*

Below them were masses of people milling about in the streets and courtyards. Into the temple court the devout were bringing animals to be sacrificed. As the smoke rose from the offerings the people bowed in prayer, imploring the God of their Fathers to bless them, to send a good market-day, good health, children to carry on the family name. Perhaps, too, they prayed for the coming of the Messiah:

Matthew
4:6

*"Jump off," he said, "and prove you are the Son of God."*

Now the devil has a lot of bad qualities, but stupidity is not one of them. He is something of a Bible scholar, it seems, and shows that he is familiar with the Old Testament prophecies about the Messiah. He even quotes one to Jesus:

Matthew
4:6

*"The Scriptures declare, 'God will send his angels to keep you from harm,' ... 'they will prevent you from smashing on the rocks below.' "*

The devil was quoting Psalm 91:12. His purpose, of course, was not to show his reliance on the authority of Scripture, but to suggest another way for Jesus to demonstrate his power. What a spectacle that would be—a man leaps off the highest point of the temple, and just before he hits the ground a legion of angels flies in to form a divine rescue net!

One of the phrases that describes the policy of the Roman emperors was "bread and circuses." This meant that the people would be content as long as they had food and entertainment. The entertainment came in many forms: gladiator duels; criminals executed publicly; lions devouring slaves; banquets; orgies. But for sheer death-defying thrills, this second suggestion of the Tempter surpasses them all. His first temptation took the form of bread, the second, circuses. But here comes the response:

Matthew
4:7

*"It also says not to put the Lord your God to a foolish test!"*

Again Jesus shows that the temptation goes far beyond a dare to jump off the temple. It is a temptation to choose a demeaning way to draw people to the kingdom of God. Such a spectacle would certainly draw a crowd, but for the wrong reason. They would come to see Jesus manipulate God, to watch Jesus command God to send his angels to the rescue. For, they thought, hadn't God promised to do so?

In that attitude lay one of the worst temptations that comes to the religious person: to put God to the test. The devil was not the only one guilty of this. He of course twisted the Scriptures he had quoted. In context, Psalm 91:12 is a promise from God, graciously and lovingly offered. On Satan's lips this gracious promise is twisted into a selfish demand. Many of the worshipers in the courtyard below were doing the same thing. The loving promises of God, given to their forefathers, they had come to take for granted, to accept as routine. Obey the rules, go through the motions, and God will deliver. After all, hasn't he promised to? They took pride in being children of Abraham, and often considered themselves innately superior to the "Gentile dogs" as they often called those unlike themselves.

The harshest words ever spoken by Jesus were directed against such hypocrisy:

Matthew 23:23, 33

*"Woe upon you, Pharisees, and you other religious leaders—hypocrites! For you tithe down to the last mint leaf in your garden, but ignore the important things—justice and mercy and faith."*

*"Snakes! Sons of vipers! How shall you escape the judgment of hell?"*

No, Jesus would not use his power to thrill the people or to put God to the test. God had indeed given him power over nature, as Jesus showed when he walked on water, when he killed a fig tree with words, but most of all, when he rose from the dead. These signs and wonders were witnessed by hundreds of people. What made believers out of some and unbelievers out of others? No simple answer suffices, but one thing cannot be overlooked: those who were most satisfied with their own lives, and had the most to lose by a radical change of values, tended to be skeptical. Believers for the most part were people in need, people not afraid to admit they could use some help in cleaning up the mess they'd made of their lives.

## Getting the Story in Mind

Mark the following statements *True* or *False*.

_____ 1. *Jesus could be tempted when alone, but not in the crowded city.*

_____ 2. *Jesus did not jump because he feared the angels would not catch him.*

_____ 3. *Jesus often used his power in order to impress the masses.*

_____ 4. *The wonders Jesus performed produced faith in many successful people of his day.*

_____ 5. *The devil knew nothing of God's Word in Scripture.*

## Getting the Meaning in Hand

*What Temptation Means.* A temptation is a test of faith. If a person remains true to his faith, he passes the test or temptation. If he gives in, he fails. Below are some responses people often make, passing or failing, to temptations. Mark them as either *pass* or *fail*.

———— 1. *"I'll forgive you, but I won't forget!"*

———— 2. *"How could God do this to me; I've never done anything to deserve it."*

———— 3. *"Lord, please let me escape this trouble; but if it must come, your will be done."*

———— 4. *"There, I've done it again. There's just no hope for me."*

———— 5. *"It won't matter if I take this; nobody will know."*

———— 6. *"I've got to remember that God has promised there is no temptation too great for us to bear with his help."*

———— 7. *"Even though I've sinned, I can receive forgiveness from God."*

# 29 Why God Sent Jesus: For Power and Glory

Jesus had turned down two of the ways men use to gain influence and power: bread and circuses. Now the devil would offer him a third way, the favorite of those throughout history who have sought to build a kingdom, to rule the world.

Matthew
4:8, 9

*Satan took him to the peak of a very high mountain and showed him the nations of the world and all their glory. "I'll give it all to you," he said, "if you will only kneel and worship me."*

Was it not the purpose of the Messiah to bring the kingdom of God to all the earth? Here is the chance to do so, the devil says. After all, is not the devil called "the Prince of this world"? Doesn't he have the power to make Jesus the next Caesar? As ruler of the world, think of the good Jesus could have done. His law would surpass the Roman law, his peace would surpass the enforced Roman peace. He could live in a manner befitting the Messiah, with all the glory and power he so rightly deserved: palaces and servants, armies to protect him, stables of the finest horses, rich clothes imported from all over the empire.

The devil of course neglected to tell how an empire would be gained and maintained. He says nothing about running roughshod over the feelings of others, friends as well as enemies; crushing the helpless under the wheels of war chariots; extorting wealth through threats and blackmail; treating humans as pawns in games of diplomacy. This was raw power the devil was offering, power without justice or love.

In his reply, Jesus rejects both the offer of power and the means to gain that power:

Matthew
4:10
*"Get out of here, Satan. The Scriptures say, 'Worship only the Lord God. Obey only him.' "*

The devil is not, in the long run, the king of this world. Jesus was choosing between the short run and the long run. And in the long run, it was God, Creator and Sustainer of the universe, the Lord and Father of mankind, who was in control. The kingdom and the power and the glory belonged to God. The power of the devil only appears to be real, only seems to be lasting. The kingdom of God on the other hand, appears to be weakness and defeat in this world. This was the reality Jesus was facing out there in the desert, early in his ministry. It was the choice he would follow as he walked among men, speaking words of wisdom and encouragement, performing deeds of compassion and forgiveness. It was the choice he would hold to, even to the very end.

These temptations never completely left Jesus, for the Gospel writer Luke ends his account of this encounter by saying,

Luke
4:13
*When the devil had ended all the temptations, he left Jesus for a while.*

More than once the people tried to make Jesus their king. Once near the end of his life, when he entered the city gates of Jerusalem, they ran before him shouting, "Hosanna to the Son of David," ready to anoint him as King in the ancient manner. Even as he rode a little donkey through the streets, Jesus looked less like a conquering hero than a humble servant of God.

His enemies had him arrested and accused him of trying to overthrow the established powers, but at his trial Jesus answered, "My kingdom is not of this world."

Even the temptation to call for legions of angels to protect him, even this temptation came back to him as the mob was taking him away to certain death. But Jesus passed the test, saying,

Matthew
26:52b-54

*"Those using swords will get killed. Don't you realize that I could ask my Father for thousands of angels to protect us, and he would send them instantly? But if I did, how would the Scriptures be fulfilled that describe what is happening now?"*

Sentenced to death by crucifixion, Jesus watched men make a mockery of his kingdom, shoving a crown of thorns on his head, a robe across his beaten and bleeding back, lifting him up nailed to a cross, to die an agonizing death between two thieves.

## Getting the Story in Mind

Check the phrase that best completes each sentence:

1 *In his third temptation, Satan offered*
_____ *a. to make Jesus ruler of the world.*
_____ *b. to bow down and worship Jesus.*
_____ *c. all the money and riches he wished.*

2 *The price to be paid for Satan's offer was*
_____ *a. nothing; the offer was free for the taking.*
_____ *b. to change his allegiance from God to Satan.*
_____ *c. to let the end justify the means.*

3 *If Jesus had accepted Satan's offer*
_____ *a. he could have built a better world.*
_____ *b. he might not have had to die.*
_____ *c. he would have given up the idea of the kingdom of God.*

4 *Jesus' refusal of Satan's offer of the kingdoms of the world meant that*
_____ *a. Satan's claim to world rule was left unchallenged.*

_____ b. *politics is of Satan.*
_____ c. *Jesus would choose another way to destroy the power of evil.*

5 *Once the temptations were ended,*
_____ a. *Satan left Jesus, never to return.*
_____ b. *Jesus claimed victory over Satan.*
_____ c. *Satan would again test Jesus' reliance on God.*

## Getting the Meaning in Hand

*More Test of Your Faith.* Suppose you were offered the chance to become "king of the world." On the left below are some possible "selling points" the devil might use, and on the right are some replies you might be able to make to each one, quoting from Scripture as Jesus did. Match the selling points with the appropriate replies.

_____ 1. *You could insulate your-self from all sadness and suffering.*

_____ 2. *Think of the wealth that would be yours.*

_____ 3. *You could easily declare war on any enemy.*

_____ 4. *You would be in control of great territory.*

_____ 5. *We'll create an image of justice and goodness for you.*

a. *Humble men are very fortunate, for the King-dom of Heaven is given to them.*

b. *Those who mourn are for-tunate! They shall be comforted.*

c. *The meek and lowly are fortunate! The whole world belongs to them.*

d. *Happy are those who long to be just and good, for they shall be completely satisfied.*

e. *Happy are those who strive for peace–they shall be called the sons of God.*

## Side Trip

To get some idea of what power struggles were like in the first century, consult a history of the Roman Empire. You may wish to choose one of the readily available histories below.

Edward Gibbon, *Decline and Fall of the Roman Empire*

# 145 *WHY GOD SENT JESUS: FOR POWER AND GLORY*

Arnold Toynbee, *A Study of History*

Will Durant, *Christ and Caesar*

Flavius Josephus, *History of the Jewish War Against Rome*
(A Jewish historian born a few years after the death of Christ, Josephus has written one of the great eyewitness accounts of life in the Empire.)

# 30 Why God Sent Jesus: For Death and Resurrection

The taunts and the tests and the temptations did not cease, even when Jesus hung dying upon the cross. *"If you are the Son of God,"* the mockers said, "come down from the cross and save yourself." How much like the devil in the desert were these human enemies beneath his cross, even to the very words they used!

Jesus could have turned the stones into bread for the people. That would have brought them streaming into the kingdom by the millions. He could have jumped off the temple into the arms of angels, drawing crowds that would hang on every word he uttered. He could have led a political revolution and a military conquest, bringing whole nations into the kingdom, even against their wills. But there he was, forsaken by all but those closest to him, while the crowd, even the religious leaders, demanded a show of power:

Matthew 27:42, 43    *"So you are the King of Israel, are you? Come down from the cross and we'll believe you! He trusted God—let God show his approval by delivering him! Didn't he say, 'I am God's Son'?"*

Jesus of course did not come down from the cross. To many, he must have seemed a great hoax, a religious false teacher, even a blasphemer. For the claims that he made about himself were not the things ordinary men say about themselves. During the course of Jesus' ministry, people had heard him say, for example, "If you have seen me, you have seen the Father." They heard him say, "I am the Way, the Truth and the Life. No one comes to the Father except through me." Jesus also said to them, "I am the bread of life; he who comes to me shall never hunger, and he that believes in me shall never thirst." Another time he said, "Heaven and earth shall pass away, but my words shall not pass away."

No, it was impossible to be neutral about Jesus. People could not accept him as just another prophet or priest or king. Not even Abraham or Moses, David or Jeremiah had made the claims about themselves that Jesus had made. People were forced to decide for or against him. It is not surprising that some decided against him, and had him put to death.

If the story of Jesus had ended with his death on the cross, we too might accept this verdict about him. We might put him in the category with other famous men whose lives were mixtures of greatness and madness, men like Van Gogh, Beethoven, Edgar Allan Poe. But the earliest followers of Jesus tell us much more. They tell us that after three days in the tomb, Jesus rose from the dead, that he appeared to his followers, spoke with them, sometimes with as many as 500 at once. These encounters were not claimed as mere seances, for they describe him eating and drinking with them, going fishing, walking, teaching them. Then one day, they tell us, Jesus "ascended into heaven."

As soon as Jesus' followers began to proclaim the good news of the resurrection of Jesus, their enemies tried to discredit them. "They have stolen the body and hidden it," the enemies claimed, even though they knew it couldn't be true, having themselves seen to it that guards were stationed at the tomb and an official seal placed across the door. They tried by threats, torture, persecution, and execution to force Jesus' followers to recant. But suffering actually strengthened the believers in their faith.

The death, resurrection, and ascension of Jesus is the

decisive event in the religion of the Bible. Those who are convinced that death is the strongest of all powers have been forced to decide against biblical religion. But those who would believe that the power of divine love is stronger even than death have found comfort, inspiration, a source of spiritual strength and hope in that belief. To every man who confronts the story of Jesus comes the time for an ultimate decision—to believe in the power of love or the power of death.

## Getting the Story in Mind

Check five ideas that describe best God's purposes in sending Jesus into the world.

_____ 1. *To show divine love for people by feeding and healing them.*
_____ 2. *To control people's minds by feeding their bodies.*
_____ 3. *To forgive those who are overcome by their own guilt and failure.*
_____ 4. *To demonstrate that God is ultimately in control of the world.*
_____ 5. *To frighten people through feats of magic.*
_____ 6. *To command people to be good.*
_____ 7. *To establish a kingdom "not of this world."*
_____ 8. *To offer a life free of suffering and danger.*
_____ 9. *To identify with men in their most ordinary situations.*
_____ 10. *To demonstrate that love is more powerful than death by the crucifixion and resurrection of the Son of God.*

## Getting the Meaning in Hand

*God with Us.* Not everyone could see God's plan in sending Jesus into the world. If Jesus had come into our modern world, we might see some newspaper headlines like those below at left, to describe the events listed below at right. Match the event with the headline "describing" it:

_____ 1. *THREE CRIMINALS*     *a. claims of divinity*
        *EXECUTED TODAY*     *b. crucifixion*
_____ 2. *CLAIMS OF SEEING*     *c. resurrection*
        *DEAD MAN ALIVE*     *d. appearances*
        *SOAR PAST 500 MARK*     *e. ascension*
_____ 3. *NEW 'PROPHET'*
        *STIRS UP MASSES*

———— *4. FOLLOWERS CEASE*
*CLAIMS OF SEEING*
*DEAD MAN ALIVE;*
*'HE IS IN HEAVEN'*
*THEY SAY*

———— *5. THREE-DAY-OLD TOMB*
*FOUND EMPTY:*
*OFFICIAL SEARCH*
*FOR BODY BEGINS*

## Side Trip

The crucifixion of Jesus has produced the most profound response through the centuries of any event in history. The art and literature of each generation has found in the Cross the most challenging subject matter of all. Familiarize yourself—perhaps begin a book or picture collection—with the greatest works of art that depict the death of Christ.

One might consider however that the greatest works of art created by Jesus have been reformed human beings, and begin instead a collection of statements by ordinary people revealing the effect of the "beautiful Savior" upon their lives.

## 25 The Old Way Ends, The New Way Begins

*GETTING THE STORY IN MIND*
1  True
2  True
3  True
4  False
5  True
6  False
7  False
8  True

*GETTING THE MEANING IN HAND*
1  c
2  b
3  c

## 26 People in Search of Salvation

*GETTING THE STORY IN MIND*
1  True
2  False
3  True
4  False
5  True
6  True
7  False
8  True
9  False
10  True

## 27 Why God Sent Jesus: For Feeding and Healing

*GETTING THE STORY IN MIND*
1  False *(Matthew 4:1-10)*
2  False *(Matthew 4:1)*
3  True *(Matthew 4:1)*
4  False *(Matthew 4:2-4)*
5  False *(Mark 6:30-44)*
6  True *(Matthew 4:4)*
7  True *(Matthew 4:4)*

*GETTING THE MEANING IN HAND*
Numbers 3 and 6

## 28 Why God Sent Jesus: For Signs and Wonders

*GETTING THE STORY IN MIND*
1  False *(Matthew 4:5, 6)*
2  False *(Matthew 4:6, 7)*
3  False *(Matthew 4:5, 6)*
4  True *(Matthew 23:23)*
5  False *(Matthew 4:6)*

*GETTING THE MEANING IN HAND*
1  fail
2  fail
3  pass
4  fail
5  fail
6  pass
7  pass

## 29 Why God Sent Jesus: For Power and Glory

*GETTING THE STORY IN MIND*
1  a *(Matthew 4:8, 9)*
2  b *(Matthew 4:9)*
3  c *(Matthew 4:10)*
4  c *(Matthew 4:12-17)*
5  c *(Luke 4:13)*

*GETTING THE MEANING IN HAND*
1  b *(Matthew 5:4)*
2  a *(Matthew 5:3)*
3  e *(Matthew 5:9)*
4  c *(Matthew 5:5)*
5  d *(Matthew 5:6)*

## 30 Why God Sent Jesus: For Death and Resurrection

*GETTING THE STORY IN MIND*
1, 3, 4, 7, 9, 10 (any five of these six are correct)

*GETTING THE MEANING IN HAND*
1  b
2  d
3  a
4  e
5  c

## How Did You Do?

| | |
|---|---|
| 40-35 | You have an excellent grasp of the life of Jesus. Have you ever thought about being his disciple? Or a teacher? |
| 34-30 | Very good. But remember, even the Devil knew a lot of facts about Jesus. |
| 29-25 | Satisfactory. You have some knowledge to share with others, but you should be encouraged to keep going. |
| 24-20 | Passing. Tempted to give up? Don't— improvement will come with time. |
| 19, under | Maybe you're the kind of person Jesus can help the most. |

# Part Six

# JESUS

## God's Son Finds
## Believers and Opponents

# 31 Introduction to the Gospels: Why There Are Four

Our impression of Jesus depends a lot on who is talking about him. In the following pages we will see him from many angles:

—A man who is blind from birth, after being healed by Jesus, has a story of joy to tell. Some Pharisees, who thought the man had been born blind because of some evil his parents had done, suspected Jesus of being in league with the devil.

—A hardened and sophisticated Samaritan woman, married five times, declared that Jesus had told her everything she ever did, and told the town that he was indeed the Messiah.

—A wealthy and powerful man, proud of his good moral record, "went sadly away," after hearing Jesus' plan for his life.

Because Jesus affected people in so many profound and fascinating ways, we are fortunate indeed that four different accounts of his life and ministry have been preserved in the Bible. The Gospel of Jesus—according to Matthew, Mark,

Luke, and John—is the theme of the first four books of the
New Testament. Each account tells enough about Jesus to
bring a man to a decision of faith. Yet each is different enough
from the others that we would suffer a great loss if any one
of them had not come down to us.

Why are there four "Gospels"? There is strictly speaking
only one gospel, one declaration of the good news of the
coming of the Messiah. Yet to look at it another way, there are
many Gospels, "according to" each of those who live and
teach the way of Christ. During the time of Jesus, and for
several years after that, there were no written records about
his life. So far as we know he never wrote anything himself.
People learned about Jesus because his followers, filled and
powered by his Spirit, told others about him.

These followers told of his life, his compassionate
words and miraculous deeds, his lowly death and
triumphant resurrection—and they told how their own lives
had been changed since they had decided to follow him. For
more than a generation, the followers of Jesus multiplied
and spread over the Roman Empire through the inspired
and inspiring testimony of these firsthand witnesses to
Jesus.

As time went on and the firsthand witnesses were being lost
through death, their testimony was collected and written
down in Greek, the common language of the day. Behind
each of the Gospels according to Matthew, Mark, Luke, and
John, stands one or more eyewitnesses. For twenty centuries
these four accounts of the Gospel were copied and recopied so
that today we are still given the same privilege as those
early believers who heard trustworthy testimony about
the coming of the Messiah.

In our time, meticulous work on the part of those who read
the original languages has given us a number of new
translations of the New Testament in clear, simple,
beautiful English. Through the millions of copies of the
Bible, available in virtually every written language on
earth, more people today may hear the gospel than in any age
in history—including the time of Jesus himself!

The writers of the four Gospels, like all the other writers
of the Bible, try not to get in the way of the story they are
telling. In contrast to many modern writers, the ancients

were uninterested in publicity, in seeing their names in print. We don't even know who wrote many of the books of the Bible. The few references to their methods that they left us become especially valuable. A brief but important explanation comes from the writer Luke in the opening words of his Gospel:

Luke 1:1-4    *Dear friend who loves God: Several biographies of Christ have already been written using as their source material the reports circulating among us from the early disciples and other eyewitnesses. However, it occurred to me that it would be well to recheck all these accounts from first to last and after thorough investigation to pass this summary on to you, to reassure you of the truth of all you were taught.*

There you have it: first the "early disciples and other eyewitnesses"—preachers who spoke the message orally to their hearers; then the writers like Luke, who first had "rechecked all these accounts from first to last"; and then compiled "this summary"; finally, the recipients like the "friend who loves God"—we know virtually nothing else about him—who must have given his priceless letter from Luke a wider circulation. It must have been read (and copies made) by small groups of believers, for later on, the Gospel According to Luke was present along with the other letters and Gospel writings in the collection of writings that make up the 27 books of the New Testament. It should not be surprising—at this stage of the course—to discover God using ordinary men and women to carry out the most earth-shaking events, like the creation of the four Gospels and the other books of Scripture. Many of those who were witnesses to the words and deeds of Jesus, many of those who preached or collected or wrote or circulated the Word of God perhaps didn't even comprehend the role they were playing in the history of the people of God. If you had asked them, "Don't you know that God is inspiring you to give his Word in the form of sacred Scripture to all the world for all time to come?" many might have simply stared at you. Whether they knew it or not, that's what happened. With the advantage of hindsight we can say of the New Testament what its own writers said of the Old Testament:

2 Timothy     *The whole Bible was given to us by inspiration from God and is*
3:16, 17     *useful to teach us what is true and to make us realize what is wrong*
*in our lives; it straightens us out and helps us do what is right. It*
*is God's way of making us well prepared at every point, fully*
*equipped to do good to everyone.*

## Getting the Story in Mind

Number the sentences below so that the story of how the four
Gospels have come down to us is placed in correct order.

_____ *Those who had known and loved Jesus told others of his
deeds and words.*

_____ *The New Testament was translated into modern languages.*

_____ *Followers of Jesus watched him and listened to him.*

_____ *The good news of Jesus spread throughout the ancient Roman
Empire by word of mouth.*

_____ *Four gospel writers drew on eyewitness accounts of Jesus' life and
wrote them down in Greek.*

_____ *The Greek versions of the Gospels were copied and recopied for
many centuries.*

## Getting the Meaning in Hand

Choose the best ending for these statements:

1    *The inspiration of Scripture is most clearly seen*

_____ *a. in the famous names of the people who wrote it.*

_____ *b. in the revealing pictures of God and man found in its pages.*

_____ *c. in the unusual means used in transmitting the words to us.*

2    *The most important factor in the formation of Scripture is*

_____ *a. the writing down of the words.*

_____ *b. the publication and circulation of books.*

_____ *c. the preservation of the oldest manuscripts.*

_____ *d. the entire process of God's actions and words in the midst of his
followers.*

3    *The written Gospels are most nearly like*

_____ *a. an on-the-spot news report.*

_____ *b. a literary fiction unrelated to real events.*

_____ *c. autobiography.*

_____ *d. a collection of eyewitness testimony.*

4 To have four accounts of Jesus' life
_____ a. is unnecessary, since they all say the same thing.
_____ b. is confusing, since they are all so different.
_____ c. is enriching, since they each give a different person's view of
Jesus.

## Side Trip

*How the Bible Came to Us.* We've spent most of our time in the course up to now concentrating on the important events and personalities of the Bible. We've said very little about how these events were transmitted through the centuries to our day—though that's also a fascinating story: how accounts of the events were handed down by word of mouth and in writings; how the various writings came to be part of the collection of sacred Scripture (and how a lot of other writings fell by the wayside in the process); how Scripture was preserved for nearly 1500 years in painstakingly handwritten copies, and for the last 500 years in printed texts and translations.

People who spend a lifetime in careful scientific study of this process often specialize in certain areas. Here are a few of the areas that might interest you. Most Bible encyclopedias and dictionaries have articles on these topics:

1. *archaeology*—a search for evidence of the actual events of the biblical world—buildings and artifacts buried beneath the sands.

2. *form criticism*—an attempt to get at the period between the events themselves and written accounts of the events—the period when the accounts were handed down by word of mouth; the writings themselves sometimes bear clues of an earlier, oral form.

3. *literary criticism*—careful analysis to determine which of the various types of literature in the Bible any given portion actually is: is it history, poetry, prophecy, legal document, material used in worship? Many tragic confusions have resulted through the years by treating poetic parts of the Bible as though they were historical, and vice versa.

4. *textual criticism*—study of the very earliest copies of the Bible still in existence, comparing them with one

another to get at an exact replica of the originals—none of which have survived.

NOTE: The word "criticism" is used by biblical scholars to mean careful critique, examination, analysis. It doesn't mean fault-finding or disparagement. Some people have indeed used biblical criticism to try to prove their own preconceptions, but such use is not scientific and does not stand the test of time.

5. *interpretation*—the principles for making the ancient Word of God clear and meaningful in our life and time.

6. *authority*—how and in what ways the Bible is the sustaining power in the lives of the believers.

7. *inspiration*—the Scripture's declarations that its authors did not merely produce human writings, but were specially inspired and empowered by the Spirit of God.

# 32 Simple Trusting Faith /
## *Jesus and the Man Blind from Birth*

Jesus tried, in many vivid word-pictures of himself, to reveal to ordinary people who he was, where he had come from, and why he had come. Once he described himself as a door, through which people could enter a new relationship with God. A shepherd who searches for lost sheep, a vine with many branches, bread sent down from heaven—in these and many other ways we see Jesus, through the eyes of the Gospel-writer, John.

One day Jesus was being challenged by the Pharisees, who disputed those who were calling Jesus a prophet. Jesus drew another word-picture:

John 8:12    *"I am the Light of the world. So if you follow me, you won't be stumbling through the darkness, for living light will flood your path."*

These words set off a furious debate. Who or what gave Jesus the right to talk like that, they demanded to know.

Some of the legal experts referred obscurely to a law that held
testimony to be valid only when two witnesses were
present. So Jesus produced two witnesses for them:

John
8:18
*"I am one witness and my Father who sent me is the other."*

That set off an even more fruitless argument about who
Jesus' father was. Jesus did not at this time say, "My
Father is God," or "I am the Son of God," but it should have
been unmistakable to his listeners who the "Father" was that
Jesus referred to.

Giving up hope that words could demonstrate his
identity, Jesus turned to actions to show that he had come
to give the "light of life" to men in darkness.

As the small group of Jesus' followers left, the Pharisees
were furious and ready to kill. Soon Jesus and the others
passed by a beggar, a man blind since birth. Jesus' disciples
reflected their own background when they asked him,
"Why was this man born blind? Was it a result of his own
sins or those of his parents?" (John 9:1)

They had the idea, popular in ancient times, that suffering
and disease were punishment sent by God for evils done by
those who suffered. You can see that such an idea was a
roadblock to compassion, and a hindrance to advances in
healing methods, for if God was the cause of the suffering, a
healer might be suspected of opposing God! Instead of being
told the correct position on the issue, we are led to a deeper
understanding of suffering:

John
9:3
*"Neither," Jesus answered. "But to demonstrate the power of
God."*

God's power was displayed, then, in curing people, not
in causing them to suffer. One of the signs of the follower of
God would be loving service:

John
9:4
*"All of us must quickly carry out the tasks assigned us by the one
who sent me, for there is little time left before the night falls and all
work comes to an end."*

Underlining the urgency of compassion, Jesus warned of
the day when men's deeds on behalf of the needy (or lack of

them) would be a basis for judgment. Making himself an example to his followers, Jesus told them,

John
9:5

*"But while I am still here in the world, I give it my light."*

Then with a dramatic gesture he showed beyond doubt that God was the power behind healing:

John
9:6, 7

*Then he spat on the ground and made mud from the spittle and smoothed the mud over the blind man's eyes, and told him, "Go and wash in the Pool of Siloam" (the word "Siloam" means "Sent"). So the man went where he was sent and washed and came back seeing!*

The Gospel according to John records the astonishment of the man's neighbors and those who were accustomed to seeing him begging. They asked the man, "How were your eyes opened?" and his answer was simple, factual, and direct:

John
9:11

*"A man they call Jesus made mud and smoothed it over my eyes and told me to go to the Pool of Siloam and wash off the mud. I did, and I can see!"*

The Pharisees heard about the healing, and their reaction was different. They accused Jesus of breaking the law. Breaking the law? A law that makes it a crime to heal a blind man? What kind of a law is that?

## Getting the Story in Mind

Check the best ending to these statements:

1 *The word-picture best describing Jesus as he healed the blind man would be*
_____ *a. the light of life.*
_____ *b. the good shepherd.*
_____ *c. bread from heaven.*

2 *The Pharisees in this story were people who*
_____ *a. recognized the power of God working in their own situation.*
_____ *b. believed the greatest commandments to be love of God and love of your neighbor.*
_____ *c. obeyed and enforced the laws of God as they saw them.*

3 *When the disciples first saw the blind man, they thought his blindness was*
_____ *a. punishment for his or his parents' wrongdoing.*
_____ *b. an opportunity to show the power of God in healing.*
_____ *c. proof that there is no God.*

4 *When following Jesus' words and example today, a person will*
_____ *a. avoid people who have gotten themselves into trouble.*
_____ *b. help people solve their spiritual problems, rather than their physical ones.*
_____ *c. try to heal suffering both physical and spiritual.*

## Getting the Meaning in Hand

Jesus found it necessary on some occasions to break, or at least suspend, the rules of his day in the name of a higher law of love. If such actions are necessary, they are also dangerous. How do you feel about rules? To find out, write one of these four words, *seldom, sometimes, often,* or *usually,* in the blank beside each question:

_____ *a. Do rules defeat the purpose for which they are made?*
_____ *b. Do law-abiding citizens ignore or even cause injustices in their community?*
_____ *c. Do churches argue about points of doctrine while ignoring people who need their help?*
_____ *d. Do school rules get in the way of learning?*
_____ *e. Do office rules get in the way of working?*
_____ *f. Do hospital rules get in the way of healing?*
_____ *g. Should good people associate with people who fall short of their moral standards?*
_____ *h. Do welfare systems put rules ahead of helping people?*
_____ *i. Are law and order the best indicators of a healthy society?*
_____ *j. Should a person obey laws which violate his conscience?*

# 33 Simple Faith Made Complicated / *Jesus and the Man Blind from Birth*

The confrontation between the man born blind and his Pharisee critics is too vivid to need much comment. Jesus was not even present. The healed beggar was on his own, facing a battery of legal and religious experts. Not even his parents stood by him. Let's just follow the story:

John
9:13-34

*They took the man to the Pharisees. Now as it happened, this all occurred on a Sabbath. Then the Pharisees asked him all about it. So he told them how Jesus had smoothed the mud over his eyes, and when it was washed away, he could see!*

*Some of them said, "Then this fellow Jesus is not from God, because he is working on the Sabbath."*

*Others said, "But how could an ordinary sinner do such miracles?" So there was a deep division of opinion among them.*

*Then the Pharisees turned on the man who had been blind and demanded, "This man who opened your eyes—who do you say he is?"*

*"I think he must be a prophet sent from God," the man replied.*

*The Jewish leaders wouldn't believe he had been blind, until
they called in his parents and asked them, "Is this your son?
Was he born blind? If so, how can he see?"*

*His parents replied, "We know this is our son and that he was
born blind, but we don't know what happened to make him see, or
who did it. He is old enough to speak for himself. Ask him."*

*They said this in fear of the Jewish leaders who had
announced that anyone saying Jesus was the Messiah would be
excommunicated.*

*So for the second time they called in the man who had been blind
and told him, "Give the glory to God, not to Jesus, for we know
Jesus is an evil person."*

*"I don't know whether he is good or bad," the man replied,
"but I know this: I was blind, and now I see!"*

*"But what did he do?" they asked. "How did he heal you?"*

*"Look!" the man exclaimed. "I told you once; didn't you
listen? Why do you want to hear it again? Do you want to
become his disciples too?"*

*Then they cursed him and said, "You are his disciple, but we
are disciples of Moses. We know God has spoken to Moses, but as
for this fellow, we don't know anything about him."*

*"Why, that's very strange!" the man replied. "He can heal
blind men, and yet you don't know anything about him! Well,
God doesn't listen to evil men, but he has open ears to those who
worship him and do his will. Since the world began there has never
been anyone who could open the eyes of someone born blind. If
this man were not from God, he couldn't do it."*

*"You illegitimate bastard, you!" they shouted. "Are you
trying to teach us?" And they threw him out.*

Then they expelled him from the synagogue. The lines were
beginning to be drawn. On one side were those like the
beggar who accepted a mysterious wonder of God in simple
trusting faith. On the other side were those like the
Pharisees, ignoring an act of compassion while trapped in
their own red tape and legalism. After the beggar had faced
the tests of the Pharisees, he was sought out by Jesus once
more:

John
9:35-38    *When Jesus heard what had happened, he found the man and
said, "Do you believe in the Messiah?"*

> The man answered, "Who is he, sir, for I want to."
> "You have seen him," Jesus said, "and he is speaking to you!"
> "Yes, Lord," the man said, "I believe!" And he worshiped Jesus.

Summarizing his mission to the world in only a few simple words, Jesus told the beggar,

John 9:39
> "I have come into the world to give sight to those who are spiritually blind and to show those who think they see that they are blind."

Which was the greater miracle? Which was the greater revelation of Jesus' divine power—*removing* the beggar's blindness, or *exposing* the Pharisees' blindness? As the personalities go their separate ways, the beggar, the Pharisees, the neighbors, Jesus, his followers, the debate continues, echoing down the corridors of time:

John 10:20-21
> Some of them said, "He has a demon or else is crazy. Why listen to a man like that?"
> Others said, "This doesn't sound to us like a man possessed by a demon! Can a demon open the eyes of blind men?"

## Getting the Story in Mind

Mark the following statements *True* or *False*.

_____ 1. Jesus healed the blind man on the Sabbath or day of rest.

_____ 2. The Pharisees agreed among themselves that healing on the Sabbath was wrong.

_____ 3. The beggar was afraid to say that Jesus had healed him.

_____ 4. The beggar's parents said they did not know who healed their son.

_____ 5. The Pharisees wanted to find out whether Jesus was the Messiah.

_____ 6. The beggar believed that Jesus had healed him through the power of God.

_____ 7. The Pharisees believed that they already knew the will of God.

_____ 8. The Pharisees invited the beggar to speak next Sabbath to the synagogue audience.

_____ 9. After the beggar was barred from the synagogue, he never saw Jesus again.

_____ 10. It was easy for anyone who saw Jesus to believe that he was sent from God.

## Getting the Meaning in Hand

Beside each of the following biblical ideas write *E* or *H* according to whether you consider it *easy* or *hard* to believe:

_____ 1. God is greater than time and space.

_____ 2. God is everywhere in everything.

_____ 3. God is good.

_____ 4. God is in control of history.

_____ 5. God spoke through Moses.

_____ 6. God sent Jesus.

_____ 7. Jesus is the Messiah promised in Scripture.

_____ 8. The wonders Jesus did were told of by those who saw them happen.

_____ 9. Jesus is the light of the world even now.

_____ 10. Jesus can open your eyes to a new life.

# 34 The Untouchables Touched / Jesus and the Samaritan Woman

If the Pharisees could find fault with Jesus because he performed works of compassion on the Sabbath day of rest, just imagine what they would have said about this: Jesus crossed racial and religious barriers to sit and talk with a woman who had a bad reputation!

The encounter might never have happened had Jesus followed all the customs of his day. He and his disciples had been in Judea, the southern region of Palestine, when they decided they needed to travel to Galilee, in the north. Now between the two regions lay the land of Samaria. You may recall that Samaria was the name of the capital city of the Kingdom of Israel after the people of God had been split in two following the reign of King Solomon. You may also remember that this northern kingdom was captured by the Assyrians in 722 B.C., more than 150 years before the Kingdom of Judah was captured by Babylon. For centuries the descendants of these two ancient kingdoms had despised one another. Each called the other an inferior race. They

refused to touch each other. They had laws against eating in
the same place. Each claimed that its own manner of worship
was more pleasing to God than the other's was. When the Jews
in Judea wanted to go back and forth to Galilee, they
avoided traveling through Samaria, even though it meant
going out of their way to the east along the Jordan River.

Jesus, however, raised eyebrows by taking the direct route
through Samaria. About midway in his journey, Jesus and his
disciples stopped to eat at the town of Sychar. Nearby lay an
ancient well, dating back hundreds of years to the time of
Jacob. Since Jacob was the grandson of the patriarch
Abraham, and the father of twelve sons whose names
identified the twelve tribes, the site of Jacob's well was
revered by both Jews and Samaritans. The well symbolized
the time long before the quarrels and wars and hatreds,
back when Jews and Samaritans were spiritual brethren. To
Jesus, the water symbolized a way in which they might
become brethren again.

Jesus was sitting by the well, and his followers had gone
to town to buy food, when a Samaritan woman came to
draw water. Jesus asked her for a drink. The woman
recognized that Jesus was a Jew, and was shocked at his
request. Then Jesus told her,

John
4:10
*"If you only knew what a wonderful gift God has for you, and
who I am, you would ask me for some living water!"*

By "living water" the Samaritan woman assumed he
meant "running water," to be found at the bottom of the
well. She observed the obvious:

John
4:11
*"You don't have a rope or a bucket, and this is a very deep well!
Where would you get this living water?"*

**But here is what he really meant by living water:**

John
4:13, 14
*Jesus replied that people soon became thirsty again after
drinking this water. "But the water I give them," he said,
"becomes a perpetual spring within them, watering them
forever with eternal life."*

Still taking him to mean drinking water, the woman answers
a little sarcastically:

John
4:15

*"Please, sir, ... give me some of that water! Then I'll never be thirsty again and won't have to make this long trip out here every day."*

But Jesus is talking about a much deeper thirst. He tries a different approach. He tells the woman to go and call her husband and return with him. When she answers that she has no husband, Jesus startles her with this insight:

John
4:17, 18

*"All too true! For you have had five husbands, and you aren't even married to the man you're living with now."*

How could he know such personal information about her, a complete stranger? She immediately confesses,

John
4:19

*"You must be a prophet."*

Perhaps the conversation was becoming too embarrassing for her, for she immediately directs attention away from herself to something more abstract, the long-standing religious differences between Jews and Samaritans:

John
4:20

*"Tell me, why is it that you Jews insist that Jerusalem is the only place of worship, while we Samaritans claim it is here [at Mount Gerazim], where our ancestors worshiped?"*

Jesus takes this state of affairs and directs it back to her own spiritual needs:

John
4:21-23

*"The time is coming, when we will no longer be concerned about whether to worship the Father here or in Jerusalem. For it's not where we worship that counts, but how we worship—is our worship spiritual and real?"*

That kind of talk seemed over her head, and the woman said she hoped some day somebody would straighten out all these complicated things:

John
4:25

*"Well, at least I know that the Messiah will come—the one they call Christ—and when he does, he will explain everything to us."*

Jesus answers,

John
4:26

*"I am the Messiah!"*

We are not told whether the woman believed that Jesus was the Messiah she had been looking for. We are told, however, that she led others to him:

John
4:28-30

*Then the woman left her waterpot beside the well and went back to the village and told everyone, "Come and meet a man who told me everything I ever did! Can this be the Messiah?" So the people came streaming from the village to see him.*

Later, after the people had heard Jesus and experienced his presence, we read that

John
4:39

*Many from the Samaritan village believed he was the Messiah because of the woman's report: "He told me everything I ever did."*

Jesus never judged anyone as an unlikely prospect for faith in him. A beggar blind from birth, even an outcast woman, were among those who brought others to faith.

Soon we will find that some who might appear on the surface to have all the qualifications of a good follower of Jesus down deep seem to feel that God needs them more than they need God.

## Getting the Story in Mind

Choose the best ending for the following statements:

1 *In showing the way of God to other men, Jesus*
———— *a. avoided the company of sinners.*
———— *b. carefully observed the customs of his day.*
———— *c. defended the Jerusalem temple as the right place to worship God.*
———— *d. none of the above.*

2 *The relationship between Jews and Samaritans had been*
———— *a. peace and brotherhood since the time of Jacob.*
———— *b. fighting and rivalry for centuries.*
———— *c. strained by religious division.*
———— *d. both b and c.*

3 *By "living water" Jesus meant*
———— *a. running water at the bottom of the well.*

_____ *b. magic water to quench thirst permanently.*
_____ *c. a spiritual resource from God.*
_____ *d. none of the above.*

4 *The woman reacted to Jesus' claim of messiahship by*
_____ *a. becoming embarrassed and running away.*
_____ *b. laughing.*
_____ *c. telling her neighbors about him.*
_____ *d. worshiping at his feet.*

## Getting the Meaning in Hand

*Why the Messiah Came.* Check the statements that give a reason for the coming of the Messiah, as revealed in the story of the Samaritan woman:

_____ 1. *To give people an escape from the world.*
_____ 2. *To list the moral rules people should live by.*
_____ 3. *To give people an inner source of spiritual strength.*
_____ 4. *To settle the religious arguments of the day by telling who was right and who was wrong.*
_____ 5. *To replace the quarreling spirit among religious people with a true spirit of reverence.*
_____ 6. *To identify with people in all conditions of life.*
_____ 7. *To demand that people bow before his power and glory.*

# 35 The "Good Prospect" Turns Away / Jesus and the Rich Young Ruler

The blind beggar and the Samaritan woman might not have seemed to us likely prospects for followers of Jesus, yet Jesus himself saw something in them not visible on the outside.

One time there came to him a successful young man who was actually seeking to be his follower. The man ran up and kneeled before Jesus, saying,

Luke
18:18

*"Good sir, what shall I do to get to heaven?"*

What a splendid opportunity this was! Here is a sincere seeker after God, and, the Bible says, a wealthy and respected leader as well. If he could be drawn to Jesus, think what good he could do: he might be able, for example, to set up a fund to provide Jesus and his followers with food, clothing, and shelter as they carried on their ministry. Certainly the man could use his influence among the others in the ruling class.

Jesus' reply to the young man is surprising and disturbing, seemingly even rude:

Luke
18:19

*"Do you realize what you are saying when you call me 'good'? Only God is truly good, and no one else."*

Then Jesus gave the standard answer people in that day gave to the question of how to obtain eternal life:

Luke
18:20

*"You know what the ten commandments say—don't commit adultery, don't murder, don't steal, don't lie, honor your parents, and so on."*

Perhaps the man was startled that Jesus' message is no more original than that. The young man answers, probably quite honestly:

Luke
18:21

*"I've obeyed every one of these laws since I was a small child."*

It is quite possible that the young man indeed had never killed, stolen, lied, or mistreated his parents or his wife. It is likely that he had grown up in a religious home where his parents taught him to obey the ancient Ten Commandments given by God through Moses to his people. If his family, of the ruling class, had been a member of the Sadducee group like so many other wealthy people of that day, they would have disapproved of the Pharisees, with their complicated interpretations of the Law. Even more than other religious people in Palestine, they would have stressed obedience to the simple commandments.

Jesus knew that it was possible to keep a few commandments, even to take pride in maintaining the ancient traditions, yet without giving one's heart and soul entirely to God. So Jesus offered the rich young man a test:

Luke
18:22

*"There is still one thing you lack," Jesus said. "Sell all you have and give the money to the poor—it will become treasure for you in heaven—and come, follow me."*

If the man had loved God above everything else, he could have given up his wealth. If he had desired the riches of heaven more than the riches of earth, he could have become

Jesus' disciple. If he had been willing, as was his ancestor Abraham, to give up even his own son, the Lord might not have required that he acqually do so. But the man showed his real motives when he flinched at Jesus' test:

Luke 18:23 *When the man heard this he went sadly away, for he was very rich.*

Jesus knew that those who had the most to give up would be least likely to show interest in the kingdom of God, and he says sorrowfully:

Luke 18:24, 25 *"How hard it is for the rich to enter the Kingdom of God! It is easier for a camel to go through the eye of a needle than for a rich man to enter the Kingdom of God."*

Even those who were not particularly wealthy were stung by this. Even the poor knew how much they envied the rich, how much they knew they would try to get rich if they could. And they asked, in despair,

Luke 18:26 *"If it is that hard, how can anyone be saved?"*

Here is the question of the ages: who can be saved? What kind of person, what kind of behavior, what kind of human life, is so good that God in his holiness and righteousness and justice can approve? Jesus shows that no man, without divine help, is acceptable. In the face of this impossibility of salvation on man's part, Jesus offers this assurance:

Luke 18:27 *"God can do what men can't!"*

## Getting the Story in Mind

Choose the best ending for these statements:

1 *In this story the man who came to Jesus was*
_____ *a. a law-abiding and influential man.*
_____ *b. a poor blind man.*
_____ *c. an immoral man.*

2 To the man's first question, "What must I do?" Jesus told him
_____ a. to give Jesus one-tenth of all he had.
_____ b. obey the law.
_____ c. tell his friends about Jesus.

3 To this the man replied that
_____ a. it was too hard.
_____ b. he would do it right away.
_____ c. he had already done that.

4 In exchange for eternal life, the man did not want to give up
_____ a. his only son.
_____ b. his immoral behavior.
_____ c. his wealth.

5 To some less affluent people who watched the rich man turn away, Jesus said
_____ a. only with God's help can any person be saved.
_____ b. only the poor can be saved.
_____ c. only people who obey God's laws can be saved.

## Getting the Meaning in Hand

Who Can Be Saved? In light of the story of the rich man's encounter with Jesus, mark five of the following statements about salvation most in harmony with Jesus' teaching.

_____ 1. Salvation depends on obedience to the Ten Commandments.
_____ 2. Salvation depends on a person's willingness to do whatever God says.
_____ 3. To be saved one must sell everything he has and give it to the poor.
_____ 4. To be saved one must turn over everything he has to God.
_____ 5. To be saved one must love the Lord with all his heart.
_____ 6. We can judge who will or will not be saved on the basis of their outward appearance.
_____ 7. God is the ultimate judge of a person's salvation.
_____ 8. Salvation is primarily a matter of a person's willpower.
_____ 9. Only through the mercy of God can any person be acceptable to him.
_____ 10. God has planned for only a few people to be saved.

## Side Trip

The story of Jesus's encounter with the rich ruler gives us a
basic principle in the teaching of Jesus on salvation. For
more specific teachings of Jesus on the subject see his
conversation with another ruler in the Gospel of John,
chapter 3, or some of his last conversations with his
disciples. Some examples are: Mark 8:31—9:1; Mark 14:22-25;
Matthew 28:16-20.

# 36 Jesus Addresses Great Crowds / *The Sermon on the Mount* *Matthew 5–7*

Jesus spent a lot of his time talking to individuals, and in the company of small groups. The man whose blindness he healed, the woman at the well, the rich young ruler, all had personal conversations with him. One of these individuals readily believed in Jesus; one was deeply impressed but perhaps not to the point of commitment; one "went sadly away."

There were hundreds of others, though, who only got to see Jesus from a distance. Even a glimpse was enough to produce faith in many of these spectators.

Imagine yourself among the crowds scattered over the hillside, straining to hear the words of Jesus. Positioning himself so the people can hear him, he begins to speak:

Matthew 5:3 *"Humble men are very fortunate! for the Kingdom of Heaven is given to them."*

If these were the only words you ever heard from the lips of Jesus, they would be enough to reveal the heart of his message. True blessedness, true happiness, Jesus says, belongs to those who are humble. Perhaps we can see now why a blind beggar was able to find his way into the kingdom of God while a rich ruler did not; why an immoral woman recognized the Messiah while some of the official religious leaders did not.

Would these words of Jesus be more familiar if they came to you in an older translation? Perhaps you recognize the words as coming from the part of the Bible that begins, "Blessed are the poor in spirit...." These are widely known as the "Beatitudes," Jesus' description of ways that lead to happiness. They are the opening words of the most famous part of the Bible, the "Sermon on the Mount." We are privileged to sit in the convenience of home and pore over these words again and again. The earliest hearers could not, so Jesus had to make his message clear and bright, like flashes from the facets of a diamond.

The Sermon on the Mount begins in Matthew chapter five and ends in chapter seven. Like people in every age, Jesus' hearers want to know who can find true happiness. In the "Beatitudes," Jesus answers: those who are humble; those who mourn; the meek and lowly; those who long to be just and good; the kind and merciful; those whose hearts are pure; those who strive for peace; those who are reviled, persecuted, and lied about. Quite a different list from those smiling faces we see in advertisements and commercials, shouting about how happy we should be because of a miraculous new ingredient in floor wax or an ineffable new color for a sports car.

Jesus continues with some words about behavior and attitudes in the old days and the new:

Matthew 5:38, 39 — *"The law of Moses says, 'If a man gouges out another's eye, he must pay with his own eye. If a tooth gets knocked out, knock out the tooth of the one who did it.' But I say: Don't resist violence! If you are slapped on one cheek, turn the other too."*

Outward obedience to laws is not the highest goal, Jesus says, but an inner spirit of love and justice:

Matthew 5:44, 45 — *"Love your enemies! Pray for those who persecute you! In that way you will be acting as true sons of your Father in heaven."*

Matthew 6:5    In chapter six we find Jesus' graphic contrasts between this genuine spiritual faith and the hollow counterfeit he so often found plaguing people's lives. "When you pray," he counseled, "don't be like the hypocrites who pretend piety by praying publicly on street corners and in the synagogues where everyone can see them." Instead, Jesus bids followers to pray simply, without pretense, along these lines:

Matthew 6:9-13    *"Our Father in heaven, we honor your holy name. We ask that your kingdom will come now. May your will be done here on earth, just as it is in heaven. Give us our food again today, as usual, and forgive us our sins, just as we have forgiven those who have sinned against us. Don't bring us into temptation, but deliver us from the Evil One. Amen."*

Even so beautiful a petition as this might become a mumbling monotony, the very opposite of the simple expression of gratitude it was originally intended to be. The religion of Jesus is not so much concerned with set rituals as it is with the condition of the soul. "Don't be anxious about tomorrow," Jesus said. "God will take care of your tomorrow too." These words provide a fitting close to his teaching about prayer in chapter six.

In chapter seven Jesus takes common, everyday subjects and shows how they can point to a higher spiritual reality. Never again can we take ordinary things for granted after we find out what Jesus has to say, for example, about specks of sawdust and great planks of wood; pearls and pigs; stones and snakes; narrow and wide gates; sheep and wolves; fruit trees and briars; houses built on rock foundations and houses built on sand.

Through the centuries, millions have found that the Sermon on the Mount offers an inexhaustible supply of spiritual pleasure and power. Treat it as you would a favorite recipe or form of recreation: the more you use it, the better it gets.

## Getting the Story in Mind

Put these sayings of Jesus back together again by matching the endings at the right with the beginnings at left:

_____ 1. "Humble men are very fortunate ..."

_____ 2. "The law of Moses says ..."

_____ 3. "Love your enemies! Pray for those who persecute you!"

_____ 4. "Don't bring us into temptation ..."

_____ 5. "Don't be anxious about tomorrow ..."

_____ 6. "Forgive us our sins ..."

_____ 7. "When you pray ..."

_____ 8. "If you are slapped on one cheek ..."

_____ 9. "They pretend piety by praying ..."

_____ 10. "First get rid of the board."

a. "... but deliver us from the Evil One."

b. "God will take care of your tomorrow too."

c. ... the Kingdom of Heaven is given to them."

d. " ... as we have forgiven those who have sinned against us."

e. "Only in that way will you be acting as true sons of your Father in heaven."

f. "But I say ..."

g. " ... turn the other too."

h. "Then you can see to help your brother."

i. "don't be like the hypocrites."

j. " ... where everyone can see them."

## Getting the Meaning in Hand

_Seeing the Extraordinary in the Ordinary._ **The seventh chapter of Matthew contains a number of common objects that Jesus used to teach spiritual lessons. Some of them are listed below at left. Match them with the lessons they teach, summarized on the right. Warning: three of the objects were not mentioned by Jesus, but are common to us and might be selected if he were living today.**

_____ 1. specks of sawdust and planks of wood

_____ 2. pearls and pigs

_____ 3. stones and snakes

_____ 4. genuine and counterfeit money

_____ 5. narrow and wide gates

_____ 6. crabgrass in a lawn

a. Don't waste your time arguing with people who don't appreciate serious matters.

b. The Christian life is not easy.

c. Watch out for people who only pretend to follow God.

d. A person's actions often reveal his values in life.

_____ 7. sheep and wolves

_____ 8. fruit trees and briars

_____ 9. freeways and country roads

_____ 10. rock and sand

e. The false often looks like the true.

f. Just when you think you have a bad habit rooted out, it springs to life again.

g. Look at your own short-comings before you criticize others.

h. Take the road less traveled by.

i. Words without actions make a weak religion.

j. God will deliver what he promises.

## 31  Introduction to the Gospels: Why There are Four

*GETTING THE STORY IN MIND*
The correct numbering: 2, 6, 1, 3, 4, 5

*GETTING THE MEANING IN HAND*
1  b *(Hebrews 1:1, 2)*
2  d *(2 Timothy 3:16)*
3  d *(Luke 1:1)*
4  c *(John 20:30, 31)*

## 32  Simple Trusting Faith

*GETTING THE STORY IN MIND*
1  a *(John 8:12)*
2  c *(John 9:16)*
3  a *(John 9:2)*
4  c *(John 9:6, 7, 39)*

*GETTING THE MEANING IN HAND*
To find your score, count 1 point for each question you answered *Seldom*, 2 points for each *Sometimes*, 3 for each *Often*, and 4 for each *Usually*. Add up the numbers for blanks *a* through *h* and put your score here: _____
Now put the scores for blanks *i* and *j* in this space: _____ and subtract. Now, finally, your score: _____ .

If your score is:

30-21   You are aware of the problem Jesus faced when he broke the Sabbath rule in order to heal the blind man.
You may also be a habitual rule-breaker, and should ask yourself, "Am I defying the norm creatively or destructively?"

20-11   You have a balanced view of the use of rules to provide a minimal norm for behavior.
You may, however, be complacent about the suffering of others, and should ask, "Am I ignoring the needs and abilities of people to whom the rules do not apply?"

10-0   You are aware of the dangers of chaos and the evils of human nature. But you may be a victim of fear and should ask yourself, "Would the world be a better place if we had more rules, or if we had more love?"

## 33  Simple Faith Made Complicated

*GETTING THE STORY IN MIND*
1  True *(John 9:16)*
2  False *(John 9:16)*
3  False *(John 9:10, 11)*
4  True *(John 9:20)*
5  False *(John 9:22, 23)*
6  True *(John 9:30)*
7  True *(John 9:28)*

8   False *(John 9:34)*
9   False *(John 9:35)*
10  False *(John 9:16)*

*GETTING THE MEANING IN HAND*
If you answered *easy* to six or more of these blanks, you probably have grown up in a religious home. But you may need to guard against taking your faith for granted.

If you answered *hard* to four or more of these ideas, you may be used to thinking mostly in the thought patterns of our own times. You may need to be more open to letting Jesus show you the world in a new light.

## 34 The Untouchables Touched

*GETTING THE STORY IN MIND*
1   d *(John 4:4-9, 21-24)*
2   d *(John 4:9, 19)*
3   c *(John 4:10-14)*
4   c *(John 4:28-30)*

*GETTING THE MEANING IN HAND*
3, 5, 6 *(John 4:14, 21-24, 7-9)*

## 35 The "Good Prospect" Turns Away

*GETTING THE STORY IN MIND*
1   a *(Luke 18:18, 21)*
2   b *(Luke 18:20)*
3   c *(Luke 18:21)*
4   c *(Luke 18:22, 23)*
5   a *(Luke 18:24-27)*

*GETTING THE MEANING IN HAND*
Numbers 2, 4, 5, 7, 9

## 36 Jesus Addresses Great Crowds

*GETTING THE STORY IN MIND*
1   c *(Matthew 5:3)*
2   f *(Matthew 5:38, 39)*
3   e *(Matthew 5:43-45)*
4   a *(Matthew 6:13)*
5   b *(Matthew 6:34)*
6   d *(Matthew 6:12)*
7   i *(Matthew 6:5)*
8   g *(Matthew 5:39)*
9   j *(Matthew 6:5)*
10  h *(Matthew 7:5)*

*GETTING THE MEANING IN HAND*
1   g *(Matthew 7:1-5)*

|    |                          |
|----|--------------------------|
| 2  | a *(Matthew 7:6)*        |
| 3  | j *(Matthew 7:7-11)*     |
| 4  | e *(Matthew 7:21)*       |
| 5  | b *(Matthew 7:13, 14)*   |
| 6  | f *(Matthew 12:43-45)*   |
| 7  | c *(Matthew 7:15)*       |
| 8  | d *(Matthew 7:16-20)*    |
| 9  | h *(Matthew 7:13, 14)*   |
| 10 | i *(Matthew 7:24-29)*    |

## *DID YOU GET THE MESSAGE?*

| | |
|---|---|
| 57-50 | Your information is that of an eyewitness. |
| 49-40 | You heard it from an eyewitness. |
| 39-30 | You've heard it, but from a distance. |
| 29-20 | Your information may be secondhand. |
| 19 or below | Perhaps you've only heard a rumor; better be careful. |

# Part Seven

# PETER

## God Sends His People
## into the World

# 37 A Fisherman Becomes a Fisher of Men / *Matthew 4*

The great epic story of the People of God that began thousands of years ago has continued through the centuries up to the present age. The story will continue till the end of time. The role you will play in this ongoing drama is still up to you. The better you understand the roles of those who have gone before, the wiser will be your decision about your own life.

Jesus Christ is the central figure in this epic. To put it another way, history is a lever and Christ is the fulcrum on which the long bar of history rests. All that came before him found its fulfillment in him, and all that ensued since him has been influenced and propelled by him. "God Sends His Son into the World"; "God's Son Finds Believers and Opponents"—perhaps these two thoughts summarize the influence of Jesus when he walked the earth. Jesus' earthly ministry was not the end of the story, of course. The believers in Jesus carried on his work. "God Sends His People into the World" and "God's People Find Believers and

Opponents"—these phrases may point the way ahead for us.

How can people like us carry on the work of Jesus? Each book in the New Testament is an answer to this question. The four "Gospels" show one way the work was carried on, as simple followers of Christ put down in writing for all time their priceless testimonies to the words and deeds of their Savior and Master. The rest of the books of the New Testament describe other believers in Jesus traveling through the world joyfully telling the good news, and tragically suffering at the hands of their enemies.

Let's look at a man who was always right at the center of things, first during the ministry of Jesus, and later as one of the leaders of the early church. His name is Simon Peter.

Probably no figure in the Bible has been subjected to as many bewilderingly different interpretations as Peter. Today's novelists and film-makers like to portray Peter as the "big fisherman," the rough-talking, impulsive, and emotional hero. Alongside this Peter we are likely to see the portrait drawn by religious leaders and painters through the centuries: this is Peter the legendary saint, the chief of Jesus' followers, the man who holds the keys to the kingdom of heaven, who passed his authority down through a succession of leaders unbroken since the beginning. Then somewhere between Peter the high and mighty, and Peter the common and lowly, we have the biblical picture of Peter the courageous preacher of the gospel of Christ and the source of practical advice about Christian living as found in the two New Testament books bearing his name.

You remember being warned that our understanding of Jesus is often clouded by traditions and legends that have grown up through the years. This warning applies again, as we look at Peter, trying to find out how the ideas and practices of Jesus were carried out by his followers. We must know how much truth there is in the popular portraits of Peter, and how much is foreign to what the New Testament says about him.

One thing we can say for sure: Jesus made a radical difference in Peter's life. The change began the first time he met Jesus:

Matthew
4:18, 19

*One day as he was walking along the beach beside the Lake of Galilee, he saw two brothers—Simon, also called Peter, and Andrew—out in a boat fishing with a net, for they were commercial fishermen.*

*Jesus called out, "Come along with me and I will show you how to fish for the souls of men!"*

And at once Peter and his brother left their nets and followed him.

There is something awe-inspiring about a man who immediately drops everything to answer the call of Jesus no questions asked, especially in contrast to the hair-splitting, self-satisfied Pharisees. We are not told whether Peter talked it over with his wife or with his partners in the fishing business. If his decision to follow Jesus was an impulsive one, it was typical of Peter's personality, as we shall soon see. And if Peter's recklessness often got him into trouble, this was one time when he made the right choice, for Jesus would turn his weakness and character flaws into powerful gifts of spiritual leadership.

## Getting the Story in Mind

Mark the following statements *True* or *False:*

_____ 1. *Jesus appointed one man as his successor.*

_____ 2. *All the followers of Jesus were appointed to carry on his work.*

_____ 3. *Peter was close to Jesus during his lifetime, but faded from the picture after the crucifixion.*

_____ 4. *Before deciding to follow Jesus, Peter had been a wealthy tax-collector.*

_____ 5. *Before deciding to follow Jesus, Peter put his business and family life in order.*

_____ 6. *The way Peter is portrayed in films, novels, and religious traditions often differs considerably from the New Testament.*

## Getting the Meaning in Hand

*Carrying on the Work of Jesus.* Some words that describe ways the work of Jesus was carried on appear at left. At right are some phrases that depict some kinds of work more specifically. Match these phrases with the appropriate words:

_____ 1. *writing*
_____ 2. *traveling*
_____ 3. *speaking*
_____ 4. *"fishing"*
_____ 5. *suffering*
_____ 6. *studying*
_____ 7. *daily living*

a. *spreading the good news*
   *throughout the world*
b. *composing the*
   *four "Gospels"*
c. *facing opposition*
   *to the gospel*
d. *casting about for*
   *people in need*
e. *preaching the message*
   *to groups*
f. *silent preaching through*
   *the quality of one's life*
g. *searching the Scriptures*

## 38 Peter the Impulsive Follower / *Matthew 14, 16, 26*

Peter believed in Jesus with all his might. He was sure that Jesus was the Messiah, the one promised by the prophets. No follower of Jesus had been more eager and enthusiastic. Sadly, though, Peter's zeal sometimes led him off in the wrong direction. So often Peter acted on impulse, with the best of intentions, only to get himself, or even his Master in trouble. Even so, Jesus never gave up on Peter. Beneath Peter's recklessness, Jesus could see a potential for the kind of spontaneity and courage that would be needed among his followers. Handled the right way Peter could become one of the great leaders of God's people.

The Gospel According to Matthew in particular sketches Peter in a way that makes all of us recognize a little of ourselves in this sincere but impulsive soul.

One episode begins when Jesus asks to be left alone to pray. Peter and some others leave him, getting into a boat and rowing across to the other shore. Perhaps they expected Jesus to cross later by land. But as they made their way, through the night, Jesus surprised them:

Matthew
14:24-27

*Night fell, and out on the lake the disciples were in trouble. For the wind had risen and they were fighting heavy seas.*

*About four o'clock in the morning Jesus came to them, walking on the water! They screamed in terror, for they thought he was a ghost.*

*But Jesus immediately spoke to them, reassuring them. "Don't be afraid!" he said.*

Now watch Peter swing into action:

Matthew
14:28-31

*"Sir, if it is really you, tell me to come over to you, walking on the water."*

*"All right," the Lord said, "come along!"*

*So Peter went over the side of the boat and walked on the water toward Jesus. But when he looked around at the high waves, he was terrified and began to sink. "Save me, Lord!" he shouted.*

*Instantly Jesus reached out his hand and rescued him. "O man of little faith," Jesus said. "Why did you doubt me?"*

If Peter hesitated in his attempt to walk across the water, he was also ready to act when the others were terrified.

On another occasion Jesus asked his followers, "Who do men say that the Son of Man is?" They gave the standard replies of the day:

Matthew
16:14

*"Some say John the Baptist; some, Elijah; some, Jeremiah or one of the other prophets."*

Then Jesus put the question directly to them:

Matthew
16:15

*"Who do you think I am?"*

It was Peter who immediately answered:

Matthew
16:16

*"The Christ, the Messiah, the Son of the living God."*

Peter was not so afraid of making mistakes that he was paralyzed to act. He was never one to hold back, nor one to stop and think overlong before acting.

For this confession of faith Jesus praises him:

Matthew
16:17

*"God has blessed you, Simon, son of Jonah,... for my Father in heaven has personally revealed this to you—this is not from any human source.*

This was one of the few times Jesus called him by his given name, Simon, son of Jonah. Usually Jesus used the name he himself had coined for his disciple—in Hebrew *Cephas,* in Greek *Peter,* in English *Rock.* Why do you suppose Jesus called this shifting-sand fisherman by the name of *Rock?* Not because he was a firm, unyielding man. And certainly not out of ridicule as unthinking people today might nickname an overweight person "Slim." No, Jesus had a plan, and the man who had just confessed him to be the Messiah would play an important part in it. Jesus explained:

Matthew
16:18, 19

*"You are Peter, a stone; and upon this rock I will build my church; and all the powers of hell shall not prevail against it. And I will give you the keys of the Kingdom of Heaven; whatever doors you lock on earth shall be locked in heaven; and whatever doors you open on earth shall be open in heaven!"*

Entrusted with great responsibility, Peter remained a fallible man, prone to mistakes, and a few days later Jesus would call the Rock a stumbling block:

Matthew
16:21-23

*From then on Jesus began to speak plainly to his disciples about going to Jerusalem, and what would happen to him there—that he would suffer at the hands of the Jewish leaders, that he would be killed, and that three days later he would be raised to life again.*
*But Peter took him aside to remonstrate with him. "Heaven forbid, sir," he said. "This is not going to happen to you!"*
*Jesus turned on Peter and said, "Get away from me, you Satan! You are a dangerous trap to me. You are thinking merely from a human point of view, and not from God's."*

Peter must have been stung by these words of censure, an almost exact mirror-image opposite of the words of blessing he had heard earlier. He was an imperfect man, but he was being won by love, deepened by training, disciplined by hardship, made useful for service by God. Nevertheless the Rock would crumble again later, during the arrest and trial of Jesus, when the mob came to take Peter's master away. Peter was right there, ready to defend him, reaching for his sword, striking out, injuring one of the crowd. Had Peter forgotten all that Jesus had said about loving the enemy? Had Jesus' own deeds of forgiveness been ignored? Probably not. But Peter's impulsiveness made it necessary for Jesus to remind him once again:

**Matthew 26:52-54**

*"Put away your sword. Those using swords will get killed. Don't you realize that I could ask my Father for thousands of angels to protect us, and he would send them instantly? But if I did, how would the Scriptures be fulfilled that describe what is happening now?*

When Peter stayed close to Jesus, his impulses could be put to good use. Separated from his Master, these same impulses could be exploited and used against him. See how the impetuous Peter reacted to ridicule, on the eve of Jesus' death:

**Matthew 26:69-75**

*Meanwhile, as Peter was sitting in the courtyard a girl came over and said to him, "You were with Jesus, for both of you are from Galilee."*

*But Peter denied it loudly. "I don't even know what you are talking about," he angrily declared.*

*Later, out by the gate, another girl noticed him and said to those standing around, "This man was with Jesus—from Nazareth."*

*Again Peter denied it, this time with an oath. "I don't even know the man," he said.*

*But after a while the men who had been standing there came over to him and said, "We know you are one of his disciples, for we can tell by your Galilean accent."*

*Peter began to curse and swear. "I don't even know the man," he said.*

*And immediately the cock crowed. Then Peter remembered what Jesus had said, "Before the cock crows, you will deny me three times." And he went away, crying bitterly.*

## Getting the Story in Mind

Choose the best ending for these sentences:

1 *Peter's usual response in the stories is*
_____ *a. act first, think about it later.*

_____ b. *think first, then act.*
_____ c. *wait for others to act first.*

2 *When Jesus invited him to walk on the water,*
_____ a. *Peter walked unafraid all the way.*
_____ b. *Peter was afraid to step out of the boat.*
_____ c. *Peter walked out onto the water, then began to sink.*

3 *When Jesus asked his disciples who they thought he was, Peter answered,*
_____ a. *"You are John the Baptist come back to life."*
_____ b. *"You are the Messiah, the Son of God."*
_____ c. *"You are one of the prophets of God."*

4 *In the evening before Jesus' death, Peter was unable to*
_____ a. *defend Jesus against the mob.*
_____ b. *stay close to Jesus during his trial.*
_____ c. *curse Jesus.*

5 *Realizing that he had been repudiating Jesus, Peter*
_____ a. *cursed.*
_____ b. *denied it.*
_____ c. *wept.*

## *Getting the Meaning in Hand*

Ten characteristics of leadership are listed below. Five of them are attributed to Peter in this lesson, five are not. Write Peter's name in the five blanks beside his particular characteristics:

1. *spontaneity* _____
2. *courage* _____
3. *training* _____
4. *enthusiasm* _____
5. *influence* _____
6. *sincerity* _____
7. *good judgment* _____
8. *patience* _____
9. *eagerness* _____
10. *experience* _____

# 39 Peter the Intrepid Leader / John 21, Acts 2:1-13

When Peter saw the suffering of Jesus, his faith wavered. When his master died the death of a criminal instead of living the life of a king, Peter seems to have lost any hope of an eventual victory. He returned to his fishing boats, as rashly as he had left them earlier.

Soon, though, the news reached him that Jesus was alive again. Peter was ready to do whatever his risen Lord would ask him. During the forty days that Jesus remained with his followers after his resurrection, he was preparing them for the work they were to do.

On one occasion the risen Lord appeared to seven of his followers as they were fishing. A strange conversation took place between Jesus and Peter:

John
21:15-17

*"Simon, son of John, do you love me more than these others?"*
*"Yes," Peter replied, "you know I am your friend."*
*"Then feed my lambs," Jesus told him.*
*Jesus repeated the question: "Simon, son of John, do you really love me?"*

> *"Yes, Lord," Peter said, "you know I am your friend."*
> *"Then take care of my sheep," Jesus said.*
> *Once more he asked him, "Simon, son of John, are you even*
> *my friend?"*
> *Peter was grieved at the way Jesus asked the question this*
> *third time. "Lord, you know my heart; you know I am," he said.*
> *Jesus said, "Then feed my little sheep."*

The three times Peter confessed his love for Jesus take us
back to his three denials of Jesus. In this dramatic way Jesus
shows he has forgiven Peter, and that he has much more in
store for him. What Peter will experience in the coming days
and years will change his life, Jesus foretells for him:

John
21:18
> *"When you were young, you were able to do as you liked and go*
> *wherever you wanted to; but when you are old, you will stretch*
> *out your hands and others will direct you and take you where*
> *you don't want to go."*

Sources outside the New Testament tell us that someone
indeed stretched out Peter's arms and bound him fast—in
crucifixion. But before this death would come, perhaps in
one of the periodic drives of the Roman emperors to wipe
out the growing Christian movement, Peter would live a
life of joyful service, feeding the sheep, the followers, of
Jesus.

It started one morning of a festival day in Jerusalem.
People had come from all over the Roman Empire to
celebrate the Feast of Weeks ("Pentecost" was the Greek
word for it), celebration of thanksgiving for the harvest.
The colorful costumes, the strange sounds of many dialects
and foreign languages, the festive air of a city where all
work stops and the music of celebration breaks out in the
streets—this was the scene of a day of Pentecost each year.

In one house, however, things were different. Some of
Jesus' closest followers were there together:

Acts
2:2-4
> *"Suddenly there was a sound like the roaring of a mighty*
> *windstorm in the skies above them and it filled the house where*
> *they were meeting. Then, what looked like flames or tongues of*
> *fire appeared and settled on their heads. And everyone present*

*was filled with the Holy Spirit and began speaking in languages they didn't know, for the Holy Spirit gave them this ability.*

The Holy Spirit of God—the same Spirit active in the creation of the world, in the creation of man himself, the same Spirit of God present with Abraham and Moses, Samuel, Saul and David, with Jeremiah and the other prophets—this divine, personal power was breaking out again in a new way.

The sound could be heard above the festival noises, and drew a large crowd to the house where the followers of Jesus had begun "to talk in other tongues":

**Acts 2:6-8**  *When they heard the roaring in the sky above the house, crowds came running to see what it was all about, and were stunned to hear their own languages being spoken by the disciples.*

*"How can this be?" they exclaimed. "For these men are all from Galilee, and yet we hear them speaking all the native languages of the lands where we were born!*

While some were perplexed and amazed at the words of praise to God that they heard, asking what it could mean,

**Acts 2:13**  *Others in the crowd were mocking. "They're drunk, that's all!" they said.*

At this, Peter raised his voice to answer them.

## Getting the Story in Mind

Use these hints from the story to fill in the missing letters of the chart below:

1   *What Jesus was doing for his disciples after his resurrection.*

2   *Peter's inmost thoughts and feelings.*

3   *Acts of Peter which made him weep.*

4   *Number of denials and number of times Jesus asked, "Do you love me, Peter?"*

5   *Peter's task as shepherd of Jesus' sheep.*

6   *The way, according to tradition, that Peter died.*

7  Source of the disciples' strange power.

8  What it sounded like when the Holy Spirit came.

9  Fiery shapes appearing on the believers' heads.

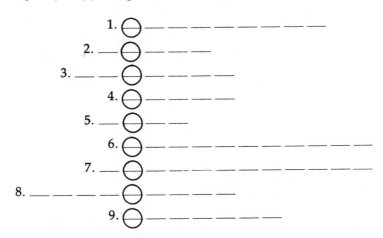

Read circled word from top down to find Greek name for
Jewish day of celebration.

## Getting the Meaning in Hand

*How Jesus Changed Peter's Life.* The death and resurrection of
Jesus were a turning point for Peter. On the left are some of
the characteristics of his old life, and on the right are some
changes Peter was enabled to make. Match the changes
with the old characteristics.

_____ 1. *resorted to violence*        *a. served others*

_____ 2. *lived as a fisherman*        *b. endured opposition,*

_____ 3. *couldn't stand ridicule*        *even to death*

_____ 4. *looked out only*        *c. became a "shepherd"*
              *for himself when*              *of God's people*
              *someone needed him*        *d. lived by the*

_____ 5. *talked first,*              *power of love*
              *thought later*        *e. spoke as the Holy*
                                        *Spirit guided him*

# 40 The New Age Begins / Acts 2:14-39

What was going on that Pentecost morning? Those people speaking in "other tongues"—were they merely drunk? As Peter begins his address to the people, he quickly disposes of this charge with a bit of sarcasm:

Acts
2:14, 15

*"Listen, all of you, visitors and residents of Jerusalem alike! Some of you are saying these men are drunk! It isn't true! It's much too early for that! People don't get drunk by 9 A.M.!"*

Then as the crowd grew serious, Peter began to explain the importance of what they were seeing and hearing. It was, he joyously declared, the great day of the Lord, so long awaited by the people of God, so long predicted by the prophets of God. He refers to a familiar prophecy from the Book of Joel:

Acts
2:17

*" 'In the last days,' God said, 'I will pour out my Holy Spirit upon all mankind, and your sons and daughters shall prophesy,*

*and your young men shall see visions, and your old men dream dreams.' "*

Great signs and wonders, miracles of nature, would be associated with this great day of the Lord, the prophecy continued. These signs, said Peter, had recently come to pass:

Acts
2:22

*"O men of Israel, listen! God publicly endorsed Jesus of Nazareth by doing tremendous miracles through him, as you well know."*

It was true that these "visitors and residents of Jerusalem alike" had heard about Jesus. Some of them, Peter charges, were part of the mob that helped get Jesus crucified:

Acts
2:23

*"But God, following his prearranged plan, let you use the Roman government to nail him to the cross and murder him."*

All Jerusalem had known about the recent killing of this "king of the Jews," and by now many of the festival visitors had been told. The sequel to this crucifixion was not so well known, so Peter continues:

Acts
2:24

*"Then God released him from the horrors of death and brought him back to life again, for death could not keep this man within its grip."*

Many could not believe in such a thing as a resurrection from the dead. Peter appeals to some words of David for proof, words like these:

Acts
2:26, 27

*" 'No wonder my heart is filled with joy and my tongue shouts his praises! For I know all will be well with me in death—*
*" 'You will not leave my soul in hell or let the body of your Holy Son decay.' "*

Then he draws this conclusion about David:

Acts
2:31

*"David was looking far into the future and predicting the Messiah's resurrection, and saying that the Messiah's soul would not be left in hell and his body would not decay."*

Bringing David's words home to the events of the day, Peter makes three points:

Acts 2:32, 33   *"He was speaking of Jesus, and we all are witnesses that Jesus rose from the dead.*

*"And now he sits on the throne of highest honor in heaven, next to God.*

*"And just as promised, the Father gave him the authority to send the Holy Spirit—with the results you are seeing and hearing today."*

The true meaning of the events of Pentecost exploded upon the listeners as Peter charged them with the terrifying truth.

Acts 2:36   *"I clearly state to everyone in Israel that God has made this Jesus you crucified to be the Lord, the Messiah!"*

Could this be true? Could this one they had seen crucified truly have been sent from God? If so, how could they live with themselves, knowing that they had rejected, even killed, the Son of God?

Acts 2:37   *These words of Peter's moved them deeply, and they said to him and to the other apostles, "Brothers, what should we do?"*

Peter's answer was direct and clear:

Acts 2:38   *"Each one of you must turn from sin, return to God, and be baptized in the name of Jesus Christ for the forgiveness of your sins; then you also shall receive this gift, the Holy Spirit."*

But Peter's answer was not restricted to those who actually helped to crucify the Son of God:

Acts 2:39   *"Christ promised him to each one of you who has been called by the Lord our God, and to your children and even to those in distant lands!"*

With that, the preaching of the Gospel of the New Age had begun. A new outpouring of spiritual power was breaking forth. The church of Jesus Christ was being born.

## Getting the Story in Mind

Mark the following statements about Peter's sermon
announcing the New Age *True* or *False:*

_____ 1. Peter said the strange babblings of the disciples were caused by
too much wine.

_____ 2. Peter told the crowd that the outpouring of God's Spirit had
been predicted in their Scriptures.

_____ 3. Peter said the wonders Jesus performed were part of the
fulfillment of prophecy.

_____ 4. Peter's audience had never heard of Jesus of Nazareth.

_____ 5. Since the people would laugh, Peter chose not to mention the
resurrection.

_____ 6. Peter said Jesus was soon to take over the ancient kingdom of
David.

_____ 7. The crowd found it easy to believe that God had allowed his son
to be crucified.

_____ 8. Peter's listeners were indifferent when they realized they had
helped to kill the Son of God.

_____ 9. Peter told them they would surely be punished for their sin.

_____ 10. The offer of repentance, baptism, and the gift of the Holy Spirit
was made mainly to those who were eyewitnesses to the
crucifixion.

## Getting the Meaning in Hand

Under each key idea about the new age of Christ, check three
phrases which help explain it.

*The Gospel:*

_____ a. Jesus has triumphed over death.

_____ b. The very Word of God has come to dwell with us.

_____ c. Salvation is restricted to those who are good enough.

_____ d. Jesus gave us a new and stricter law to obey.

_____ e. Sin, evil, suffering, and death are losing their grip.

*The Church:*

_____ a. Followers of Jesus Christ in all times and places.

_____ b. The community of those penitent believers whose baptism gave
them a new start in life and a new spiritual power.

_____ c. The new organization God has chosen to gather all the good
people out of the world.

_____ d. *A new building to replace the synagogue and the temple.*

_____ e. *Everyone whom the Lord has called to accept the offer of forgiveness.*

*The Spirit:*

_____ a. *A dangerous emotional disturbance that makes people look drunk.*

_____ b. *A gift offered by Jesus Christ and God the Father.*

_____ c. *A divine power associated with resurrection and new life.*

_____ d. *A supernatural force that always produces the miraculous.*

_____ e. *A promise to all who receive forgiveness of sins.*

# 41 The People Respond to Peter's Good News / Acts 2:41-47; Acts 4, 5, 8

It was Peter's finest hour. The persuasive power of his simple, clear conviction of God's action through Jesus, stirred the crowd to action. Though we are not given every word of this sermon, we have enough to understand why the people responded as they did:

Acts
2:41

*Those who believed Peter were baptized—about 3,000 in all!*

The immediate experience of these new believers was one of love, joy, peace, sharing, and learning together. The description of those early days has served as a model for the spiritual life of every group of Christians through the centuries, calling the people back again and again whenever the freshness of belief begins to fade:

Acts
2:42-47

*They joined with the other believers in regular attendance at the apostles' teaching sessions and at the Communion services and prayer meetings. A deep sense of awe was on them all, and the apostles did many miracles.*

*And all the believers met together constantly and shared everything with each other, selling their possessions and dividing with those in need. They worshiped together regularly at the Temple each day, met in small groups in homes for Communion, and shared their meals with great joy and thankfulness, praising God. The whole city was favorable to them, and each day God added to them all who were being saved.*

From the very beginning, this ideal was put to the test. We are reminded of Jesus and the blind man as we discover that the first opposition to the young church came from religious leaders who criticized Peter for healing a crippled man. Arrested and clapped into jail overnight, Peter and his companion John proclaimed to all who would listen the good news about the resurrection of Jesus, the sign that God indeed had sent him as the Messiah. The impression Peter and John left on the hearers is memorable:

Acts
4:13
*When the Council saw the boldness of Peter and John, and could see that they were obviously uneducated non-professionals, they were amazed and realized what being with Jesus had done for them!*

Along with the attacks from outside came some subversion from within. Along with the generous sharing of most of the believers came a selfish and glory-seeking act on the part of a couple named Ananias and Sapphira. Apparently they sold a piece of land and gave a sizable sum of money to the church, claiming it was the full amount received for the land, when actually they were keeping part of it for themselves. Their sin was not lack of generosity, but hypocrisy. The sudden death of this couple caused a sense of fear and awe, perhaps also a new sense of closeness, among the members of the church.

Peter and the others had to face the agonizing situation of being ordered by religious and political leaders to stop preaching in the name of Christ. Peter's simple answer has given courage to martyrs through the ages who have died for their faith. He told the leaders:

Acts
5:29
*"We must obey God rather than men."*

There were, of course, great occasions of joy as well. The baptism of the first believer from Africa must have been such an occasion. He was a eunuch, treasurer to the queen of Ethiopia, and his contact with the message of Christ came during a chariot ride, when a young servant of God named Philip climbed aboard. The Ethiopian treasurer knew the story of God's people as told in the Scriptures, so Philip explained how Jesus was the one to whom the prophets had pointed. The man was convinced:

Acts
8:36-39

*As they rode along, they came to a small body of water, and the eunuch said, "Look! Water! Why can't I be baptized?"*

*"You can," Philip answered, "if you believe with all your heart."*

*And the eunuch replied, "I believe that Jesus Christ is the Son of God."*

*He stopped the chariot, and they went down into the water and Philip baptized him. And when they came up out of the water, the Spirit of the Lord caught away Philip, and the eunuch never saw him again, but went on his way rejoicing.*

The good news was beginning to spread: among the Jews visiting in Jerusalem, to African travelers, and soon to Greeks and Romans.

## Getting the Story in Mind

Choose the best ending for the following sentences:

1 *Those who accepted Peter's Pentecost sermon*
_____ *a. were given an examination.*
_____ *b. were baptized.*
_____ *c. refused Peter's counsel.*

2 *Soon after Peter's sermon, the small groups of Jesus' followers*
_____ *a. were almost destroyed by persecution.*
_____ *b. grew to over 3,000 persons.*
_____ *c. converted most of the other citizens of Jerusalem.*

3 *The early disciples in Jerusalem met for worship*
_____ *a. secretly in their homes.*
_____ *b. once a week in their own place of assembly.*
_____ *c. daily, sometimes in homes, sometimes in public places.*

4 *Drawn by their faith, the followers of Jesus*
_____ *a. shared their possessions to care for the poor among them.*
_____ *b. avoided contact with sinful people outside their group.*
_____ *c. had few problems.*

5 *In the early days, Christianity began to spread*
_____ *a. primarily among friends and relatives.*
_____ *b. into Africa and Europe.*
_____ *c. wherever gullible people could be found.*

## Getting the Meaning in Hand

With the early church in Jerusalem as a model, check the five qualities most to be hoped for in a church today:

_____ 1. *willingness of members to visit in each others' homes.*
_____ 2. *spontaneous joy in praising God.*
_____ 3. *enough wealth to build comfortable buildings to meet in.*
_____ 4. *a confidence that they knew all they needed of God's Word.*
_____ 5. *ability to expose hypocrisy and error in the community.*
_____ 6. *generally favorable impression in the local community.*
_____ 7. *a uniformity of class and social background.*
_____ 8. *the sharing of each according to his ability to each according to his need.*
_____ 9. *harmonious relations with the local political authorities.*
_____ 10. *daily growth in numerical and spiritual strength.*

# 42 Early Growth and Persecution / *Acts 10, 11*

Those who had prided themselves in the glorious past were unable to accept the new acts of God in their own day. The gospel message would have to find a hearing instead among the Gentiles, the so-called outsiders.

Such an outsider was Cornelius, a military officer in the Italian regiment. He is described as

Acts
10:2

*a godly man, deeply reverent, as was his entire household. He gave generously to charity and was a man of prayer.*

It would become Peter's privilege to announce the good news of salvation to Cornelius. But Peter had some growing up to do before he could preach to Cornelius. You see, all his life Peter had been taught that Gentiles like Cornelius were members of an inferior race, not to be spoken to or associated with. Through long centuries of preoccupation with their own survival, the People of God had all but forgotten the ancient promises of God to the patriarchs, that

"all the nations of the earth" would be blessed. They
underplayed the old idea that God created all mankind in
his own image; they neglected the message of the
prophets that God had chosen his People for a special
mission to all nations, and not because the chosen ones were
better than everybody else. Jesus reached back into the past,
dusted off these ancient teachings and put them into
practice. He taught and ministered to all kinds of people,
breaking through the barriers between Jew and Samaritan,
between rich and poor, respectable and outcast, traditional
and progressive. Even in death, his Cross became an
international symbol, the inscription fastened to it being
written in Hebrew, Latin, and Greek. After his
resurrection, Jesus made clear his commission to go to all
nations:

Matthew
28:18-20

*"I have been given all authority in heaven and earth. Therefore
go and make disciples in all the nations, baptizing them into the
name of the Father and of the Son and of the Holy Spirit, and
then teach these new disciples to obey all the commands I have
given you; and be sure of this—that I am with you always, even
to the end of the world."*

To the ends of the earth till the end of time—those were the
borders of Jesus' concern. His followers heard the
command but were slow in beginning to execute it. In the
case of Peter, God had to send a vision to show him Gentiles
were not to be considered unholy or untouchable. Upon
receiving the invitation to go to the home of Cornelius,
Peter saw the meaning of the vision:

Acts
10:25-28

*As Peter entered his home, Cornelius fell to the floor before him
in worship.*

*But Peter said, "Stand up! I'm not a god!"*

*So he got up and they talked together for a while and then
went in where the others were assembled.*

*Peter told them, "You know it is against the Jewish laws for me
to come into a Gentile home like this. But God has shown me in a
vision that I should never think of anyone as inferior.*

Cornelius explained how he had come to invite Peter, and
how he wanted to hear Peter's message, so Peter began:

Acts
10:34, 35

*"I see very clearly that the Jews are not God's only favorites! In every nation he has those who worship him and do good deeds and are acceptable to him."*

Then Peter told the people about Jesus, in much the same way he spoke on the day of Pentecost, saying "he went about doing good and healing all who were oppressed by the devil." Citing his own personal experiences—"We can bear witness to all that he did in the Jewish countryside and in Jerusalem"—Peter told them of Jesus' cruel death and victorious resurrection, his appearance to many witnesses, declaring that

Acts
10:43

*"all the prophets have written about him, saying that everyone who believes in him will have their sins forgiven through his name."*

The rest of the story is a kind of Gentile version of Pentecost, with the power of the Holy Spirit descending upon the people, and their baptism in water in the name of Jesus Christ:

Acts
10:44-48

*Even as Peter was saying these things, the Holy Spirit fell upon all those listening! The Jews who came with Peter were amazed that the gift of the Holy Spirit would be given to Gentiles too! But there could be no doubt about it, for they heard them speaking in tongues and praising God.*
*Peter asked, "Can anyone object to my baptizing them, now that they have received the Holy Spirit just as we did?" So he did, baptizing them in the name of Jesus, the Messiah.*

In Peter's two messages, the one on Pentecost and the one to Cornelius' household, there were some differences and some basic similarities.

To the people in Jerusalem, some of whom may actually have been part of the mob that shouted, "Crucify him, crucify him!" Peter was like a prosecuting attorney holding before them the chilling picture of "this Jesus, whom you crucified." It was enough to strike the conscience of many, and Peter told them to "repent."

To the large household of Cornelius, who was described as "generous," "religious," and "prayerful," Peter tells the same story of how God sent Jesus, but he spends much less time on the guilt of his hearers and much more time showing how God's actions break down the boundaries that for years seemed to exclude Gentiles like Cornelius.

On Pentecost, Peter promised the gift of the Holy Spirit to all who penitently submitted to baptism into Christ. In Cornelius' house, Peter was still speaking when the gift of the Holy Spirit was poured out.

Peter was not troubled by the different ways God chose to work in the two situations. As he explained later to some Jewish Christians who wanted to know why he allowed Gentiles to be baptized into Christ,

Acts 11:17
*"Since it was God who gave these Gentiles the same gift he gave us when we believed on the Lord Jesus Christ, who was I to argue?"*

That satisfied the questioners. They concluded God knew what he was doing:

Acts 11:18
*When the others heard this, all their objections were answered and they began praising God! "Yes," they said, "God has given to the Gentiles, too, the privilege of turning to him and receiving eternal life!"*

They might also have quoted the old passage from Samuel:

1 Samuel 16:7
*"Men judge by outward appearance, but I look at a man's thoughts and intentions."*

## Getting the Story in Mind

Compare Peter's message on Pentecost with his message to Cornelius's household. Mark the following references to his sermons either *P* for Pentecost or *C* for Cornelius. (Warning: some references are so similar in both cases that you may have to refer carefully to the text.)

_____ 1. *a prophecy, familiar to Jews, from the book of Joel*
_____ 2. *"God has shown me in a vision that I should never think of anyone as inferior."*
_____ 3. *"God publicly endorsed Jesus of Nazareth by doing tremendous miracles through him."*
_____ 4. *"In every nation he has those who worship him and do good deeds and are acceptable to him."*

_____ 5. "God ... let you use the Roman government to nail him to the cross and murder him."

_____ 6. "He went around doing good...."

_____ 7. "We all are witnesses that Jesus rose from the dead."

_____ 8. "We apostles are witnesses of all he did throughout Israel and in Jerusalem."

_____ 9. "this Jesus you crucified"

_____ 10. Jesus' cruel death, victorious resurrection, and appearances to many witnesses

Compare the people's response on Pentecost with the response in Cornelius' household, again marking the occasion *P* or *C*:

_____ 1. "These words of Peter's moved them deeply."

_____ 2. "fell before him in worship"

_____ 3. "Stand up! I'm not a god!"

_____ 4. "Brothers, what should we do?"

_____ 5. "Turn from sin, return to God, and be baptized."

_____ 6. "Then you shall receive this gift, the Holy Spirit."

_____ 7. "Even as Peter was saying these things, the Holy Spirit fell upon all those listening!"

_____ 8. "Can anyone object to my baptizing them, now that they have received the Holy Spirit just as we did?"

_____ 9. "Those who believed Peter were baptized."

_____ 10. "It was God who gave these Gentiles the same gift he gave us when we believed."

_____ 11. "They joined with other believers in regular attendance at the apostles' teaching sessions and at the communion services and prayer meetings."

_____ 12. "God has given to the Gentiles, too, the privilege of turning to him."

## Getting the Meaning in Hand

*Why People Turn to Christ.* A lot of the problems people in the first century found answered when they became followers of Jesus are needs people still have today. Below is a list of some of these needs. Mark any of them that are especially acute in your own life.

_____ 1. A need for more evidence that belief in God is valid.

_____ 2. A more meaningful relationship with people close to you.

_____ 3. *A need to communicate real religious values to your children.*

_____ 4. *A need to express secret doubts no one knows you have.*

_____ 5. *A need to feel completely accepted and forgiven.*

_____ 6. *A need to get out from under some controlling habit.*

_____ 7. *A need to stop living only to make more and more money.*

_____ 8. *A need to get out of recurring spells of depression.*

_____ 9. *A need to cross barriers to other people, erected by race, creed, nationality, age, social status, or education.*

_____ 10. *A need to experience the reality of God's presence today.*

_____ 11. *A need to be a part of a community of loving people.*

_____ 12. *A need to conquer fear of death.*

_____ 13. *A need to find out what following Jesus would mean in your life.*

_____ 14. *A need to overcome some of the wrongs and injustices you see in the world.*

_____ 15. *A need to give of your best to serve others.*

## 37 A Fisherman Becomes a Fisher of Men

*GETTING THE STORY IN MIND*
1 False *(Matthew 16:18, 19)*
2 True *(Matthew 28:18-20)*
3 False *(John 21)*
4 False *(Matthew 4:18)*
5 False *(Matthew 4:19, 20)*
6 True *(Matthew 4:18-20; 14:24-32;*
     *16:15-23; 26:69-75)*

*GETTING THE MEANING IN HAND*
1 b *(Luke 1:1-4)*
2 a *(Acts 8:4)*
3 e *(Acts 2:40)*
4 d *(Matthew 4:19, 20)*
5 c *(Acts 4:18, 19)*
6 g *(Acts 17:11)*
7 f *(1 Peter 3:1, 2)*

## 38 Peter the Impulsive Follower

*GETTING THE STORY IN MIND*
1 a *(Matthew 14:28, 29; 16:16, 22)*
2 c *(Matthew 14:28-30)*
3 b *(Matthew 16:15, 16)*
4 b *(Matthew 26:57)*
5 c *(Matthew 26:75)*

*GETTING THE MEANING IN HAND*
Peter's characteristics:
1. spontaneity; 2. courage; 4. enthusiasm; 6. sincerity; 9. eagerness

## 39 Peter the Intrepid Leader

*GETTING THE STORY IN MIND*

| | | |
|---|---|---|
| 1. | P reparing | *(John 21, especially verses 17-22)* |
| 2. | h E art | *(John 21:17)* |
| 3. | de N ials | *(Luke 22:56, 57)* |
| 4. | T hree | *(Matthew 26:69-75; John 21:15-17)* |
| 5. | f E ed | *(John 21:15-17)* |
| 6. | C rucifixion | *(John 21:18)* |
| 7. | h O ly spirit | *(Acts 2:4)* |
| 8. | wind S torm | *(Acts 2:2)* |
| 9. | T ongues | *(Acts 2:3)* |
| | PENTECOST | *(Acts 2:1)* |

*GETTING THE MEANING IN HAND*
1 d *(John 18:10; Acts 6:40, 41; 11:1-18)*
2 c *(Matthew 4:18; John 21:17)*
3 b *(Matthew 26:69-74; Acts 5:28, 29)*

4   a *(Matthew 26:69-74; Acts 4:5-8)*
5   e *(Matthew 14:28; Acts 4:8-10)*

## 40  The New Age Begins

*GETTING THE STORY IN MIND*
1   False *(Acts 2:15)*
2   True *(Acts 2:16)*
3   True *(Acts 2:22)*
4   False *(Acts 2:22, 23)*
5   False *(Acts 2:24)*
6   False *(Acts 2:29-33)*
7   False *(1 Corinthians 1:21-23)*
8   False *(Acts 2:37)*
9   False *(Acts 2:38)*
10  False *(Acts 2:39)*

*GETTING THE MEANING IN HAND*
The Gospel: a *(Acts 2:24)*; b *(Acts 2:22)*; e *(Acts 2:24)*
The Church: a *(Acts 2:39)*; b *(Acts 2:38)*; e *(Acts 2:39)*
The Spirit: b *(Acts 2:32, 33)*; c *(Acts 2:32, 33)*; e *(Acts 2:39)*

## 41  The People Respond to Peter's Good News

*GETTING THE STORY IN MIND*
1   b *(Acts 2:41)*
2   b *(Acts 2:41)*
3   c *(Acts 2:42, 46)*
4   a *(Acts 2:44, 45)*
5   b *(Acts 8:27-39)*
    *(Acts 16:9-12)*
    *(Acts 23:11)*

*GETTING THE MEANING IN MIND*
1 *(Acts 2:46)*; 2 *(Acts 2:46)*; 8 *(Acts 2:45)*; 10 *(Acts 2:47)*
(the above four are correct; fifth answer is for thought.)

## 42  Early Growth and Persecution

*GETTING THE STORY IN MIND*
Message:
1   Pentecost *(Acts 2:16-21)*
2   Cornelius *(Acts 10:28)*
3   Pentecost *(Acts 2:22)*
4   Cornelius *(Acts 10:35)*
5   Pentecost *(Acts 2:23)*
6   Cornelius *(Acts 10:38)*
7   Pentecost *(Acts 2:32)*
8   Cornelius *(Acts 10:39)*

9   Pentecost *(Acts 2:36)*
10  Cornelius *(Acts 10:39-41)*

Response:
1   Pentecost *(Acts 2:37)*
2   Cornelius *(Acts 10:25)*
3   Cornelius *(Acts 10:26)*
4   Pentecost *(Acts 2:37)*
5   Pentecost *(Acts 2:38)*
6   Pentecost *(Acts 2:38)*
7   Cornelius *(Acts 10:44)*
8   Cornelius *(Acts 10:47)*
9   Pentecost *(Acts 2:41)*
10  Cornelius *(Acts 11:17)*
11  Pentecost *(Acts 2:42)*
12  Cornelius *(Acts 11:18)*

### GETTING THE MEANING IN HAND

As far as we're concerned, God is the only one who knows how to score this test, so we can only recommend this course of action:

Pray about it. Simply ask for help. If you've never prayed much before, just go down the list and say, "Dear God, I need …" and list your needs. That's a start. Then begin looking for signs that the prayer is being answered. Some answers come quickly, some more slowly. Some (remember Abraham and Sarah?) might take a while.

### KEEPING UP WITH PETER

| | |
|---|---|
| 89-80 | You're privileged to tell the world about Jesus. |
| 79-70 | You stayed with Peter all the way to Pentecost. |
| 69-60 | You were with him when Jesus forgave him. |
| 59-50 | You were with him when he confessed his faith. |
| 49-40 | You followed him across the water, but fell in. |
| 39 and under | Still fishing. (Maybe Jesus will come along and ask you to follow him.) |

# Part Eight

# PAUL

## God's People Find
## Believers and Opponents

# 43 The Great Opponent Becomes the Great Believer / Acts 9, 22, 26

Probably the most obvious fact of life today is change. The only thing that stays the same is change. Many of the great clashes of our time are between those who want change to come gradually, without upsetting things too much, and those who want change to come quickly, sweeping away the ills of the past. Attitudes toward change pit nation against nation, fathers against sons, gradualists against revolutionaries. Much of the turmoil in the news can be understood in terms of conflicts between those who want change to be sudden and those who want it to be gradual.

For some people, commitment to Christ causes a cataclysmic change in their lives. If they have ridiculed or ignored religion, lived a callous and selfish life, a change is often triggered by some tragic or violent event—the death of a loved one, the loss of a job, a fire or flood that destroys home and possessions, experience in war.

For others, following Christ is more gradual, more natural. Reared in a religious home, taught high

standards with patience and compassion, many would
never dream of opposing the will of God as they understand
it. Even these, however, discover new insights they have
never known before, insights that make their faith more
meaningful than it has been in the past.

In the early days of Christianity, tension between sudden
change and gradual growth was focused sharply in the life of
one man. His name was Saul of Tarsus. After all the trouble
Jesus had with the Pharisees, it comes as a surprise to find
out that it was a Pharisee, of all people, who became
history's most celebrated disciple of Jesus. He wasn't just a
one-day-a-week Pharisee either. His early years, as Saul
himself later recalled, were spent doing everything he could to
stop and harass Christians:

Acts
26:10, 11

*"I imprisoned many of the saints in Jerusalem, as authorized by
the High Priests; and when they were condemned to death, I cast
my vote against them. I used torture to try to make Christians
everywhere curse Christ. I was so violently opposed to them
that I even hounded them in distant cities in foreign lands."*

Saul of Tarsus. His name hints at a lot that made him
tick—Saul, namesake of the first king of Israel; Tarsus, his
birthplace in what is now Turkey, then a seaport city
where the ancient traditions of Judaism, Greek philosophy,
and Roman law were mixed with the latest fashions of
thought and behavior.

The Jews were a minority group in Tarsus. They faced
some of the same kind of discrimination there that they
practiced in their homeland against the Samaritans. Few
Roman legal documents that come down to us from Saul's
time have a kind word to say about the Jews. The Romans
were always having to make special exceptions for them in
the imperial policy. Saul tried with all his might to resist
the pressures from the outside. Imagine then his horror
when he detected what he thought was heresy from the
inside. One day, Saul says,

Acts
22:5

*"I asked them for letters to the Jewish leaders in Damascus, with
instructions to let me bring any Christians I found to Jerusalem in
chains to be punished."*

The letters were never delivered. Instead, something happened to Saul that, to say the least, added to our language a new figure of speech: "to see the light." But let Saul himself tell about it:

Acts 22:6-8

*"As I was on the road, nearing Damascus, suddenly about noon a very bright light from heaven shone around me. And I fell to the ground and heard a voice saying to me, 'Saul, Saul, why are you persecuting me?'*

*"'Who is it speaking to me, sir?' I asked. And he replied, 'I am Jesus of Nazareth, the one you are persecuting.'"*

Before he found himself lying there on the ground hearing an unidentifiable voice, apparently there was not the slightest doubt in Saul's mind that the devil was behind the Christian movement. Jesus of Nazareth? He's the leader of a splinter group that attacked the Law and rejected the Fathers. Now in a blinding flash, Saul's former assumptions about God's will for mankind become obsolete.

The voice tells him to continue his trip to Damascus, where he will be told what is coming next. Blinded by the light, and stunned by the import of the voice, Saul groped his way into the city, assisted by his companions.

Acts 22:13

*"Brother Saul, receive your sight."*

The voice this time was that of Ananias, a fellow Jew who had come to believe in Christ. Ananias indeed tells Saul what is coming next:

Acts 22:14, 15

*"The God of our fathers has chosen you to know his will and to see the Messiah and hear him speak. You are to take his message everywhere, telling what you have seen and heard."*

Saul's mission included something to know, something to see, something to hear, and something to be. Taken altogether, they would make it possible for Christianity to grow from a tiny cell of believers in Palestine to a faith that has gone "into all the world."

Acts 22:16

*"And now, why delay? Go and be baptized, and be cleansed from your sins, calling on the name of the Lord."*

With his baptism, Saul reached a milestone in his sudden turnaround. But a conversation is not all there is to faith. Saul would spend the rest of his life gradually discovering what he gave up and what he would receive as a follower of Christ.

## Getting the Story in Mind

1 Before he turned to Christ, Saul of Tarsus was
_____ a. an atheist.
_____ b. a very strict religious person.
_____ c. a worldly, sophisticated man.

2 His earthly attitudes toward Christians led him to
_____ a. respect them.
_____ b. harass and persecute them.
_____ c. ignore them.

3 When the vision of Christ came to Saul, he was
_____ a. in a worship service.
_____ b. on his way to arrest some Christians.
_____ c. on a missionary journey.

4 When the great light came upon him, Saul
_____ a. saw Jesus himself.
_____ b. heard a voice.
_____ c. saw nothing, heard nothing.

5 Saul's first response to the vision was
_____ a. "What is this?"
_____ b. "What shall I do?"
_____ c. "Who is it?"

6 The vision made Saul
_____ a. deaf.
_____ b. dumb.
_____ c. blind.

7 When Saul arrived in Damascus, there came to him
_____ a. a fellow Jew who believed in Jesus.
_____ b. a former Jew who had given up his old ways.
_____ c. a non-Jew who believed in Jesus.

8 *Ananias told Saul*

_____ a. *God has appointed you to know his will and be his witness; arise, be baptized.*

_____ b. *God has selected you for your outstanding service; rise and receive his blessing.*

_____ c. *God has decided to punish you for your wickedness; depart into everlasting fire.*

## Getting the Meaning in Hand

*What Conversion Means.* Check the conclusions below which can rightly be drawn from the story of Saul's conversion.

_____ 1. *A person who thinks he is helping God may actually be working against him.*

_____ 2. *A person who has done wrong can still be changed by God.*

_____ 3. *A person who believes strongly in God will naturally be kind to everyone.*

_____ 4. *God is actively seeking ways to bring men back to him.*

_____ 5. *There is nothing a man can do in response to God's sovereign will.*

_____ 6. *Unless a man sees a vision, he cannot find God.*

_____ 7. *A person who "sees the light" can make a great change in life.*

# 44 The Problem of the Hyphenated Christian / *Paul's Letter to the Church at Rome*

After Saul's conversion, which to say the least was a surprise to himself, his friends, and the persecuted Christians alike, he spent a lot of time by himself trying to see what it all meant.

He wrestled with the question of how much of the old way of life was gone forever, how much would still be of value to him, and most important of all, what new possibilities his allegiance to Christ opened before him. His concern with this problem is at the core of the writings he left us. We can tell that it wasn't merely an abstract, theoretical question, but one that had to be worked out in flesh-and-blood situations. Saul of Tarsus began to see the dimensions of the problem as he traveled around, starting new communities of believers in the major cities of the eastern Mediterranean region.

The problem of what is given up and what is received by the believer differed, he found out, depending on whether the person's background was Jewish or Gentile. The new followers of Christ who grew up in Jewish homes were steeped in the ancient biblical tradition of the Law and the Prophets. Those who were from a Greek background often had been polytheists—believers in many gods, each having power over a single aspect of nature: sun, moon, war, fertility, and so on. Saul (who when traveling in Greek-speaking areas called himself by the Greek form "Paul") was quick to see the danger of the infant Christian movement being overwhelmed or diluted by the older traditions. Instead of becoming simple followers of Jesus, people might end up as hyphenated Christians—Jewish-Christians or Gentile-Christians.

One of Paul's writings in particular tries to get at the heart of the Christian faith: his letter to the Church at Rome. This letter is a masterpiece. Probably no other writing in history has been responsible for more religious reforms, and more individual conversions, than Paul's "Letter to the Romans."

Perhaps the reason people for centuries have returned to this letter to get their spiritual bearings is that in it Paul came to grips with the enduring issues of faith. In his day the greatest threat to the message Paul announced came in two forms—a way of life based on Law and a way of life based on Nature.

The way of the Pharisees that Paul had forsaken was the way of what we might call the "law-abiding citizen."

The way of the Gentiles that lay in the background of many converts was based on what we might call the principle of "doing what comes naturally."

In the case of the Jews it was the law of Moses that was to be obeyed. In the case of the Gentiles it was the law of nature, or the conscience, that was to be followed.

In our day the two choices persist. There are many people, perhaps more numerous in the older generation, for whom obedience to the law of the land is their highest allegiance. In contrast to and often in conflict with the law-abiding citizen, there are many people, often found among the younger generation, for whom the law of nature, the law of "doing what comes naturally" is their idea of a happy life. Possibly the reason so many in these generations are at each other's throats is that they haven't had a chance to hear

of a third choice. Once again Paul's letter to the Romans is
fresh as the morning news, urgent as an ambulance siren.

Paul opens his letter by taking up the nature of the
Gentile faith. He quickly agrees to the kernel of truth at the
heart of doing what comes naturally: the Gentiles are right
in saying that nature contains signs of the presence of God,
of his will for their happiness:

Romans
1:19, 20
*The truth about God is known to them instinctively; God has put
this knowledge in their hearts. Since earliest times men have seen
the earth and sky and all God made, and have known of his
existence and great eternal power. So they will have no excuse
[when they stand before God at Judgment Day].*

The world God has made—all of creation—reflects the
presence of God, Paul agrees. There is only one catch.
People have a tendency not to see God in the things he
created, but to see only the things themselves. They can't
see the proverbial forest for the trees. All sorts of trouble
result: we exalt things all out of proportion to their importance
in relation to people. People begin to love things and use
people, instead of using things and loving people—or to
use Paul's phrase for it:

Romans
1:25b
*They prayed to the things God made, but wouldn't obey the blessed
God who made these things.*

Relationships get all twisted: sexual relations become
perverted; nature itself is mistreated and polluted; love
loses its meaning.

No, says Paul, nature is not enough. It promises more than
it can deliver.

"Amen, brother Saul!" some of his readers would be
saying. "We've got a word for what you're condemning.
We call it 'idolatry.' And we have laws against idolatry. Laws
against sexual perversion. Laws against destruction of the
land. Laws against mistreating people. It's all there in the
Law of Moses, if people would only keep it faithfully."

Paul had been down that road before. His profound
analysis of this way of life can perhaps be boiled down to two
points:

Romans
2:23    *You are so proud of knowing God's laws, but you dishonor him
by breaking them.*

Those whose motto was "law and order" also broke the
law when it cut across their own desires. Secondly,

Romans
7:7    *I would never have known the sin in my heart—the evil desires
that are hidden there—if the law had not said, "You must not have
evil desires in your heart."*

In other words, the Law could point out what is wrong, but
it couldn't motivate people to follow what is right:

Romans
7:21    *It seems to be a fact of life that when I want to do what is right, I
inevitably do what is wrong.*

What Paul needed was the motivation to enjoy doing what
is best for him, and to find no pleasure in what is
destructive. That motivation is what he found in the new
way of life:

Romans
8:2    *The power of the life-giving Spirit—and this power is mine
through Christ Jesus—has freed me from the vicious circle of sin and
death.*

What is this life-giving law and how is it different from the
law of nature or written law? How can it set you free?
More about that, coming up.

## Getting the Story in Mind

Mark the following statements *True* or *False*.

_____ 1. *Saul, a man of Jewish background, used a Greek name for
himself when among Greek people.*

_____ 2. *In his letter to the Christians at Rome Paul tried to get at the
heart of the Christian faith.*

_____ 3. *As a Pharisee Saul had striven above all to obey the Law.*

_____ 4. *Paul, in* Romans, *holds that people learn nothing about God by
looking at the natural World.*

_____ 5. *Paul believes that perverted human relations arise out of
stressing material things while forgetting the Creator of all
things.*

_____ 6. *Paul believes that the best way to end bad behavior is to make a law against it.*

_____ 7. *For Paul the highest motivation for the good life is found in the spirit of Jesus Christ.*

## Getting the Meaning in Hand

*Nature, Law, and Spirit.* Try to distinguish among the three ways of life Paul talks about in Romans—the life based on nature, the life based on law, the life based on the spirit of Christ—by marking the following ideas either *nature, law,* or *spirit:*

_____ 1. *loving things and using people*

_____ 2. *doing what comes naturally*

_____ 3. *being a law-abiding citizen*

_____ 4. *"and the great thing about this deal, it's all perfectly legal."*

_____ 5. *an inner motivation to enjoy the true, the good, the beautiful*

_____ 6. *set free in order to serve*

_____ 7. *always let your conscience be your guide*

# 45 Disturber of the Peace, or Messenger of Peace? / Acts 16

Probably the best way to get an idea of the change in Paul's life after he had been "set free," motivated by "the power of the life-giving Spirit" is simply to follow him around.

That's not easy to do, for Paul never stayed very long in one place. Three times he set out from the port city of Antioch, not far from his hometown, supported by the church there, to travel through the provinces in hopes of starting groups of believers. Paul and his companions usually stayed in one place only long enough to get a group started. For further teaching of the young churches he relied on return trips, letters, and most of all, the life-giving Spirit.

Let's greet Paul as he arrives in the city of Philippi. Located in what is now northern Greece, Philippi was named after Philip of Macedon, father of Alexander the Great. We are about to see a head-on collision of the gospel of Christ and the natural religion of the Gentiles:

Acts
16:16-18
*"One day as we were going down to the place of prayer beside the river, we met a demon-possessed slave girl who was a*

*fortune-teller, and earned much money for her masters. She
followed along behind us shouting, "These men are servants of
God and they have come to tell you how to have your sins
forgiven."*

*This went on day after day until Paul, in great distress, turned
and spoke to the demon within her. "I command you in the name
of Jesus Christ to come out of her," he said. And instantly it left
her.*

Oracles, spirit-possession, fortune-telling—it all sounds
exotic or even implausible to the modern mind. Before
dismissing it, talk to someone who has been to countries
where such phenomena still are common. Because Paul set
the girl free from the evil spirit, he found himself in trouble:

Acts
16:19

*Her masters' hopes of wealth were now shattered; they grabbed
Paul and Silas and dragged them before the judges at the
marketplace.*

Apparently Paul had hit them where it hurt the hardest: not
their theology, but their pocketbook.

Acts
16:20, 21

*"These Jews are corrupting our city," they shouted. "They are
teaching the people to do things that are against the Roman laws."*

A gem of propaganda, this brief sentence. Its effect on the
crowd was predictable:

Acts
16:22-24

*A mob was quickly formed against Paul and Silas, and the judges
ordered them stripped and beaten with wooden whips. Again and
again the rods slashed down across their bared backs; and
afterwards they were thrown into prison. The jailer was
threatened with death if they escaped, so he took no chances,
but put them into the inner dungeon and clamped their feet into
the stocks.*

Behind bars did Paul lament his bleeding back and aching
ancles? Not a bit: He proceeded to gather an audience:

Acts
16:25

*Around midnight, as Paul and Silas were praying and singing
hymns to the Lord—and the other prisoners were listening...*

Paul was "set free," even in prison. In fact, he didn't need
to try to break out, even when he had a golden opportunity:

Acts
16:26, 27

*Suddenly there was a great earthquake; the prison was shaken to
its foundations, all the doors flew open—and the chains of every
prisoner fell off! The jailer wakened to see the prison doors wide
open, and assuming the prisoners had escaped, he drew his
sword to kill himself.*

Suicide would be better, the jailer thought, than certain
execution for the crime of letting prisoners escape.

Acts
16:28, 29

*But Paul yelled to him, "Don't do it! We are all here!"*
*Trembling with fear, the jailer called for lights and ran to the
dungeon and fell down before Paul and Silas.*

From what you hear of the way prison guards often treat
prisoners, this sudden turnaround by the Philippian jailer
has to be up there with the Damascus road experience of Saul
himself as one of the all-time great about-faces. Such was
the impact of Paul's conduct in the emergency (which
saved the jailer's life) that the jailer was led to an unusual
response:

Acts
16:30

*He brought them out and begged them, "Sirs, what must I do to be
saved?"*

Paul's answer was essentially that given to everyone who
asked since the days of Peter's sermon on the day of
Pentecost:

Acts
16:31

*"Believe on the Lord Jesus and you will be saved, and your entire
household."*

What followed was also consistent with the process of
becoming a Christian wherever the gospel was
preached—hearing the Word, responding in penitence,
baptism into Christ, celebration of the new life:

Acts
16:32-34

*They told him and all his household the Good News from the Lord.*
*That same hour he washed their stripes and he and all his family*
*were baptized. Then he brought them up into his house and set a*

*meal before them. How he and his household rejoiced because
all were now believers!*

As a parting shot, Paul decided to insist on his civil rights as a
Roman citizen when the city officials tried to sneak him out
of jail instead of acknowledging the mistake they had
made:

Acts
16:37

*"Oh, no they don't! They have publicly beaten us without trial and
jailed us–and we are Roman citizens! So now they want us to leave
secretly? Never! Let them come themselves and release us!"*

After seeing it in action, what can we say about this new
"law of the Spirit"? At least these things. First it is a law that
sometimes employs, sometimes transcends, and sometimes
clashes with human law. Second, being spiritual it can
make a man free even when he is behind bars. And third,
whatever else it is, it is not dull.

## Getting the Story in Mind

In the sentences below, fill in the blanks from the words in the
list.

| | | | |
|---|---|---|---|
| unfastened | prisoners | trust | demonic |
| illegal | Roman | profits | |
| immoral | imprisoned | prophets | |
| oracular | himself | Supreme | |
| baptized | private | believe | |

1   In Philippi Paul met a slave-girl possessed by a
_____ spirit.

2   The fortune-teller followed Paul and his friends for days calling
them servants of the _____ God.

3   When Paul cast the spirit out of the slave-girl, her owners were
angered by their loss of _____ .

4   The slave owners accused Paul of spreading _____
customs.

5   Without trial, Paul and Silas were beaten
and _____ .

6 While Paul and Silas prayed, an earthquake _____ all the prisoners' chains.

7 The jailer would have killed _____ if Paul had not stopped him.

8 Paul told the jailer to _____ in the Lord Jesus.

9 After the jailer was _____ he fed Paul and Silas in his own home.

10 Because they were _____ citizens Paul and Silas could insist on a public apology.

## Getting the Meaning in Hand

*The Law of the Spirit.* Match the events from the story (at left) with the qualities that describe the law of the Spirit (at right):

_____ 1. Paul shows kindness to his prison guard.

_____ 2. Paul sings hymns while in pain and in prison.

_____ 3. Paul presses for his rights as a Roman citizen.

_____ 4. Paul's adventures in spreading the gospel bring him joy and woe.

_____ 5. Paul's healing of the slave-girl cuts into her owner's profits.

a. The Law of the Spirit employs human law.

b. The Law of the Spirit transcends human law.

c. The law of the Spirit clashes with human law.

d. The Law of the Spirit frees a man though he is imprisoned.

e. The Law of the Spirit makes life meaningful and dramatic.

# 46 Letters from Prison / Colossians, Philemon

Most of us depend on the law of the land to protect us from the violent and the unscrupulous in our society. We should be sobered to remember that Joseph and Jeremiah, Peter and Paul all served time in prison. Jesus himself met his death with the consent of those who controlled the legal system.

During one of Paul's long stays in prison while awaiting trial, he used the time to deepen his own faith and to encourage others through letters. As we look at two such letters, one to a church and one to an individual, we find Paul unselfishly trying to help people work out their problems in the spirit of love.

The young churches had no certain way of verifying their belief that the way of love was the wave of the future. It certainly wasn't the wave of the present. A bewildering variety of competitors presented themselves for people's allegiance. Along with the imperial political leaders and the traditional religions, a parade of cults and sects promised salvation and union with the divine through special diets, systems of meditation, exotic rituals, abstinence programs. The church at Colosse seemed especially threatened, or at least worried, so from prison Paul writes a letter to the Colossians to help them pick their way through the competing claims.

He reminds his readers of the changes God has made in their own lives through Jesus Christ. These changes they can vouch for:

Colossians 1:13, 14    *He has rescued us out of the darkness and gloom of Satan's kingdom and brought us into the kingdom of his dear Son, who bought our freedom with his blood and forgave us all our sins.*

But Jesus Christ is not just some assistant deity in charge of customer relations. No, Paul assures them that the divine power of Christ to forgive sins is the same power that created and still is active in the whole universe:

Colossians 1:16    *Christ himself is the Creator who made everything in heaven and earth, the things we can see and the things we can't; the spirit world with its kings and kingdoms, its rulers and authorities; all were made by Christ for his own use and glory.*

This staggeringly vast vision of God's plan should draw their attention away from the petty problems of their local situation and draw them toward eternity and infinity as theaters of God's activity.

Some of the local problems that were bothering the Colossians now could be seen from a new viewpoint:

Colossians 2:16    *Don't let anyone criticize you for what you eat or drink, or for not celebrating Jewish holidays and feasts or new moon ceremonies or Sabbaths.*

There have always been people who have made certain foods and drinks, and certain holiday observances, central to their religion. There have always been others for whom the abstinence from these things becomes central. Paul tries to show them how shortsighted and trivial both attitudes are:

Colossians 2:17    *These were only temporary rules that ended when Christ came. They were only shadows of the real thing—of Christ himself.*

He also warns against the efforts of people who "try to enter into some vision of their own," whether stimulated by a drink, a plant, an artificial substance, or even by meditation or will power. In the same way, rigorous programs of abstinence are warned against:

Colossians 2:23, 24
*These rules may seem good, for rules of this kind require strong devotion and are humiliating and hard on the body, but they have no effect when it comes to conquering a person's evil thoughts and desires. They only make him proud.*

Paul knows people often cannot withdraw from such crutches simply by deciding to quit. He knows they cannot hope to escape the power of these "elemental spirits of the world" unless they first come in contact with the power of the Cross:

Colossians 3:1
*Since you became alive again, so to speak, when Christ arose from the dead, now set your sights on the rich treasures and joys of heaven.*

At the time Paul wrote to the Colossians, he prepared another letter to a wealthy slave-owner named Philemon, who was a leader in a nearby congregation. It is one of the shortest books in the Bible (one chapter, twenty-five verses), but word-for-word one of the most remarkable.

What an explosive situation it is: one of the slaves in Philemon's house has escaped with stolen money. The penalty for this crime in those barbaric days was death by wild beasts. The slave, whose name is Onesimus, has crossed paths with Paul, and has been helping Paul during his imprisonment.

The obvious thing for Paul to do is keep Onesimus and protect him. But because Paul, Onesimus, and Philemon are brothers in Christ it is possible for him to do more—to ask Philemon to take Onesimus back, to forgive him of his crime, free him from slavery, and help him to spend his life in his own chosen way of service.

Paul of course will have to be careful with his words. And he is; the letter to Philemon is a model of diplomacy.

Paul begins by identifying himself with Philemon through the bond they share in Christ:

Philemon
verse 4

*"I always thank God when I am praying for you, dear Philemon."*

He speaks of

Philemon
verse 6

*"your love and trust in the Lord Jesus and in his people."*

Though Paul has the authority as an apostle to be coercive and strict with Philemon, instead he uses compassion. His first reference to Onesimus is discreet and direct, as

Philemon
verse 10

*"my child Onesimus, whom I won to the Lord while here in my chains."*

He tells Philemon he is returning Onesimus,

Philemon
verse 12

*"and with him comes my own heart."*

He would rather that Onesimus stay with him, but he wants Philemon's decision not to be

Philemon
verse 14

*"because you had to but because you wanted to."*

Then comes the most compelling sentence of all:

Philemon
verses 15,
16a

*Perhaps you could think of it this way: that he ran away from you for a little while so that now he can be yours forever, no longer only a slave, but something much better—a beloved brother, especially to me.*

Very delicately Paul comes to the matter of the stolen money:

Philemon
verse 18

*If he has harmed you in any way or stolen anything from you, charge me for it.*

He ends the letter on a note of optimism:

Philemon
verse 21

*I've written you this letter because I am positive that you will do what I ask and even more!*

As an afterthought he adds:

Philemon
verse 22

*Please keep a guest room ready for me, for I am hoping that God will answer your prayers and let me come to you soon.*

Perhaps Paul wants to "inspect what he expects"; at any rate the combination of appeals seems irresistible.

The letter to Philemon, and all of Paul's letters from prison, lead one to suspect that Christianity has never really been tried as an alternative to oppression or revolution. It has been used to justify social injustice and violent redress (and fence-sitting compromise), but too rarely has its goal for society been achieved—forgiveness with reconciliation.

## Getting the Story in Mind

Choose the best ending to the following sentences:

1 *When Paul was put in prison, he spent much of his time*
_____ *a. trying to find a way to escape.*
_____ *b. making friends with the guards.*
_____ *c. helping other people with their problems.*
_____ *d. learning to rehabilitate himself.*

2 *The churches in Paul's day*
_____ *a. needed encouragement and faith to keep going.*
_____ *b. had plenty of evidence that they were right.*
_____ *c. were unduly upset over other religious claims.*
_____ *d. had more faith than churches in later times.*

3 *In encouraging the Colossian Christians, Paul appealed first of all to*
_____ *a. scientific evidence of the existence of God.*
_____ *b. contradictions in other religions.*
_____ *c. his authority as an apostle.*
_____ *d. the changes they can see in their own lives.*

4 *Paul shows that the power of Christ*
_____ *a. is mainly to forgive sins of individuals.*
_____ *b. is mainly to make changes in society.*
_____ *c. pervades the entirety of reality.*
_____ *d. has not yet been authorized by God.*

5 *When Paul talks about rules that ban eating, tasting, or touching certain things, he*
_____ *a. shows that Christianity is a religion of do's and don't's.*
_____ *b. warns against self-destructive programs of abstinence.*
_____ *c. lays down the rules for eating and drinking.*
_____ *d. implies that Christians do not need to discipline themselves.*

6 When Paul meets a slave who has escaped with stolen money from a Christian master, he

_____ a. returns the slave to his master for punishment.

_____ b. sends the slave out on his own.

_____ c. writes the master to come get the slave.

_____ d. tries to persuade the master to free the slave.

7 Paul's attitude toward oppressed people is

_____ a. to take no action since it is not a spiritual matter.

_____ b. to justify the oppressed person's condition as the will of God.

_____ c. to try to destroy the oppressor.

_____ d. to try to destroy oppression by freeing both oppressor and oppressed from bondage.

## Getting the Meaning in Hand

No theme pervades the biblical story more than "freedom from bondage." From the slaves in Egypt to the Christian slave Onesimus, from the imprisoned heroes of Israel to the imprisoned Apostle Paul, the goal of freedom is a rich, many-sided, even paradoxical idea. Study this lineup of people who have lost their freedom. Then answer the questions at the end of the list.

1 a teen-ager in trouble put in jail with inmates who will teach him to become an expert in crime.

2 a soldier held captive by the enemy.

3 a heroin addict or alcoholic imprisoned by his habit.

4 millions of people in Asia, Africa, and Latin America who earn less than $100 a year.

5 an invalid confined to his bed.

6 a person judged insane and committed to an asylum.

7 an outspoken writer imprisoned under a dictatorship.

8 a young man in prison for resisting the draft.

9 residents of cities where they are afraid to go out at night.

10 a man with a treadmill job he cannot escape and cannot enjoy.

11 a shy person shackled by lack of confidence.

12 *a slave of prejudice who cannot trust or love a person much different from himself.*

*Identify the prisoners from the list which fit the following descriptions.*

*Which prisoner was most like someone you know?* _____

*Which prisoner was least known to you?* _____

*Which prisoner is most like you?* _____

*Which prisoner could you help the most?* _____

# 47 Jesus Christ, Incorporated / Paul's First Letter to the Corinthians

Paul was the man who probably started, visited, and wrote to more churches than anyone else in his time. Whenever he got down to the basics of what a church really is, one idea continually floated to the surface: the church as a *body*. In fact you could almost say that for Paul the church is Jesus Christ, Incorporated. To incorporate means "to make into one body, intimately united or blended."

When talking about followers of Jesus taken as a group, Paul would rather use the word "body" than the word "church." In his first letter to the Corinthian church, for example, the "body of Christ" theme reverberates through every page like the beat of a song:

1 Corinthians 10:17    *No matter how many of us there are, we all eat from the same loaf, showing that we are all parts of the one body of Christ.*

1 Corinthians 12:27    *All of you together are the one body of Christ and each one of you is a separate and necessary part of it.*

It is clear that for Paul, unlike many in his day, the body was to be valued and respected. Otherwise he would never have used it as his favorite synonym for the people of God. The body, many believed, was the cause of sin and guilt and separation from God. It was considered inferior to the spirit. The body would die, while the spirit was eternal. Not quite so, according to Paul. He believed the body and spirit were united:

1 Corinthians
6:19
*Haven't you yet learned that your body is the home of the Holy Spirit God gave you, and that he lives within you?*

Even in death the body is not destroyed, it is transformed:

1 Corinthians
15:44, 49
*They are just human bodies at death, but when they come back to life they will be superhuman bodies. For just as there are natural, human bodies, there are also supernatural, spiritual bodies. Just as each of us now has a body like Adam's, so we shall some day have a body like Christ's.*

The body is sacred. It cannot be ignored, neglected, degraded, abused.

The Corinthian church was having a lot of problems. Most of them, Paul believed, were related to the body. Take sex for example. Many Christians in Corinth were trying to put sex down, to treat it as unimportant or inferior. Predictably all kinds of problems were shooting up. There was the case of the man who was having sexual relations with his stepmother. The Corinthians, thinking sexual matters weren't as important as being spiritual, were ignoring or even sanctioning a relationship so loaded with destructive power. Paul's counsel is to take sex and the body more seriously:

1 Corinthians
6:19b, 20
*Your own body does not belong to you. For God has bought you with a great price. So use every part of your body to give glory back to God, because he owns it.*

There were others who were trying a kind of spiritual marriage, without sexual contact. Some Christians may have been trying to avoid sexual contact with non-Christian mates, who might not be favorably impressed with that way of life.

Paul himself seemed to get along all right unmarried, though he knew not everybody could. So he does not praise the abstainers for their self-control or "spirituality," but reminds them they are not in sole possession of their own bodies:

1 Corinthians 7:4, 5a *A girl who marries no longer has full right to her own body, for her husband then has his rights to it, too; and in the same way the husband no longer has full right to his own body, for it belongs also to his wife. So do not refuse these rights to each other.*

Many of the problems in this church Paul tried to work out on the basis of the body of Christ. We will mention only two: one having to do with playing favorites in choosing leaders, and the other having to do with being self-centered while trying to worship together.

The Corinthian church had had several ministers. Each one had brought several families to Christ. Parties were forming around the memories of these preachers:

1 Corinthians 1:12 *Some of you are saying, "I am a follower of Paul"; and others say that they are for Apollos or for Peter; and some that they alone are the true followers of Christ.*

Paul sees that each minister has shared in the growth of the church, but the credit belongs to God:

1 Corinthians 3:5 *Who am I, and who is Apollos, that we should be the cause of a quarrel? Why, we're just God's servants, each of us with certain special abilities, and with our help you believed.*

There wasn't only a leadership problem, there was also a fellowship problem. When the Christians ate together, and took the Lord's Supper together, there was no real communion taking place. The parties are in fellowship within the party, but not with the rest of the church:

1 Corinthians 11:18, 19 *Everyone keeps telling me about the arguing that goes on in these meetings, and the divisions developing among you, and I can just about believe it. But I suppose you feel this is necessary so that you who are always right will become known and recognized!*

Especially in the service of communion, where the body and
blood of the Lord are commemorated, it is necessary to
prepare one's mind to commune and share with the Head
and all the other members:

1 Corinthians  *A man should examine himself carefully before eating the bread*
11:28, 29  *and drinking from the cup. For if he eats the bread and drinks from
the cup unworthily, not thinking about the body of Christ and
what it means, he is eating and drinking God's judgment upon
himself; for he is trifling with the death of Christ.*

To keep the Body of Christ sound and healthy, Paul says, there
must be both unity and variety. Unity comes from the
equilibrium provided by the Head, Jesus Christ. Variety
comes from the many different talents and personalities of
the members:

1 Corinthians  *Now God gives us many kinds of special abilities, but it is the*
12:4-6  *same Holy Spirit who is the source of them all. There are different
kinds of service to God, but it is the same Lord we are serving.
There are many ways in which God works in our lives, but it is
the same God who does the work in and through all of us who are
his.*

Every member is needed. Jesus the Head needs all the
members, and would suffer if any were cut off:

1 Corinthians  *Yes, the body has many parts, not just one part. If the foot says,*
12:14, 15, 18  *"I am not a part of the body because I am not a hand," that does not
make it any less a part of the body.
But that isn't the way God has made us. He has made many
parts for our bodies and has put each part just where he wants it.*

Each member has its own abilities, assignments, or to use
Paul's word, "gifts." There is one gift that is indispensable
to all members. Take it away, and even a healthy body
dies instantly, as though plunged into a vacuum. Here it is:

1 Corinthians  *Love is very patient and kind, never jealous or envious, never*
13:4, 5  *boastful or proud, never haughty or selfish or rude. Love does not
demand its own way. It is not irritable or touchy. It does not hold
grudges and will hardly even notice when others do it wrong.*

If God had intended to reveal to every man in history the right way to solve every problem that would arise, his Word wouldn't be able to fit in all the libraries we could build. Instead, we get dazzling glimpses of the truth in places like this letter of Paul to the Corinthians, glimpses of both the eternal principles and the day-to-day applications. It is all any Body needs to stay healthy, if it can remember:

1 Corinthians    *There are three things that remain—faith, hope, and love—and*
13:13    *the greatest of these is love.*

## Getting the Story in Mind

Choose the best ending for the following statements:

1  *When talking about followers of Jesus taken as a group, Paul prefers the word*

_____  *a. church.*

_____  *b. body.*

_____  *c. building.*

_____  *d. souls.*

2  *According to Paul, the spirit and the body are*

_____  *a. separate but equal.*

_____  *b. united.*

_____  *c. competing.*

_____  *d. evil.*

3  *Many of the Corinthians believed that sexual relations for a spiritual person were*

_____  *a. less important than "spiritual" matters.*

_____  *b. the most important aspect of life.*

_____  *c. necessary for a happy marriage.*

_____  *d. inseparable from other dimensions of life.*

4  *Paul's counsel for solving the Corinthians' sex problems is:*

_____  *a. "You are set free; all things are lawful."*

_____  *b. "Abstain as much as possible from sexual contact."*

_____  *c. "Your own body does not belong to you."*

_____  *d. "The truly spiritual person loses his sexual drives."*

5  *The main problem centered in the Lord's Supper was*

_____  *a. they weren't offered it often enough.*

_____  *b. they were having the Lord's Supper as part of a regular meal.*

_____ c. *the various parties had no real communion with the whole Body.*

_____ d. *they were more concerned with feeding the poor than with serving God.*

6 *To help solve the problem of the party spirit Paul urged that all church members*

_____ a. *join Paul's own following.*

_____ b. *agree to disagree.*

_____ c. *start a new congregation elsewhere.*

_____ d. *view each other as members of the body of Christ.*

7 *Jesus, the head of the body, the church, needs*

_____ a. *all members to do the same kind of work.*

_____ b. *only the most gifted people for members.*

_____ c. *all members to contribute their own talents for the good of the whole.*

_____ d. *no members at all, for he is the Head.*

8 *The one gift that all members of the body need is*

_____ a. *knowledge.*

_____ b. *love.*

_____ c. *organizational ability.*

_____ d. *spiritual maturity.*

## Getting the Meaning in Hand

*Keeping the Body of Christ Healthy.* At left are some diseases to which the Body of Christ is vulnerable. At right are some treatments often recommended. Match the diseases with the treatments.

_____ 1. *heart trouble: life-blood fails to circulate properly.*

a. *Regular examinations. Curable only if caught in early stages.*

_____ 2. *cancer: a malignant tumor spreads and slowly kills the Body.*

b. *Regular exercise, elimination of habits that poison the system.*

_____ 3. *respiratory ailment: the Body cannot get fresh air.*

c. *A deeply rooted conflict that may need to be traced to its origin in childhood.*

_____ 4. epilepsy: the members react convulsively, out of control.

_____ 5. schizophrenia: a split personality, responding to two conflicting sets of values.

_____ 6. appendicitis: one small organ erupts and en-dangers the life of the whole Body.

_____ 7. common cold: general weakness due to ordinary exposure to the elements.

d. Operate as soon as possible.

e. Plenty of rest and good diet can minimize this ordinary and universal ailment.

f. A different climate sometimes helps.

g. Curable only when the nervous system is brought under control of the brain.

## Side Trip

If you are a member of a Body of Christ, try to relate the above-mentioned diseases and treatments to your own situation. For which of these ailments can you find symptoms? For which ones can you prescribe treatments?

# 48 Enduring to the End / *The Book of Revelation*

If you have stayed with us all the way through the first forty-seven stops of our tour, you've come in contact with more of the biblical way of life than many people will discover in a lifetime. Before you finish, one more important discovery remains.

In many ways a journey through the biblical world seems like a trip to exotic lands of long ago and far away. It would miss the point completely to put the emphasis on the past without equal stress on the present and future. Abraham lived not for pleasant memories of the past (few of which he had) but for the future God had promised to bring to pass through the patriarch's descendants. The prophets keenly analyzed the strengths and weaknesses of their own society. They envisioned a greater future than their workaday fellow citizens could comprehend.

Nearly everything Jesus said and did referred to the future "Kingdom of God" where love and justice and righteousness would reign, when "the end" would come.

Before the end, the world would run its course of violence, bloodshed and death:

Matthew 24:6, 7    *When you hear of wars beginning, this does not signal my return; these must come, but the end is not yet. The nations and kingdoms of the earth will rise against each other and there will be famines and earthquakes in many places.*

It will be a time of a severe endurance test:

Matthew 24:13    *Those enduring to the end shall be saved.*

In the writings of the apostle Paul, what strikes the reader as the recurring theme is the coming ferocious struggle between the powers of life and the powers of death. We are living in the time between the resurrection of Christ and the rising of all the dead:

1 Corinthians 15:24    *After that the end will come when he will turn the kingdom over to God the Father, having put down all enemies of every kind.*

The end of time is a theme that for some reason seems to fascinate two kinds of people in particular: the oppressed and desperate whose lot is so wretched that they long for a new day; and the dreamers and speculators who would rather construct worlds of their own in the sky instead of grappling with the real and less tractable world in which they live. People who are more content with life as they find it often turn away from symbolic futuristic language and the effort it takes to interpret it.

To say that language is symbolic doesn't mean it can't refer to real things. Just as a $1000 bill is a cheap piece of paper symbolizing real buying power, the biblical language of the future is a human set of words reaching for a transcendant reality.

The longest portion of the Bible written in this symbolic language comes not from the prophets or Jesus or Paul, but from a servant of Christ named John, called the Seer or Revelator. His work is called the Apocalypse or Book of Revelation.

To many modern readers the Book of Revelation is the most difficult part of the Bible. Some people spend years advancing farfetched theories to explain it. Others avoid it like the plague. Neither the fanaticism nor the boycott is really necessary.

The Book of Revelation is a drama. The main character is God; the plot reveals "what must shortly happen" to the church and to the whole earth. It is a drama that actually follows the structure of a play script: seven acts, each with seven scenes. Here is a synopsis:

| | |
|---|---|
| Prologue | (Chapter 1) |
| Act I | Reading of Letters to Seven Churches (Chapters 2, 3) |
| Act II | Opening of Seven Seals (Chapters 4-7) |
| Act III | Sounding of Seven Trumpets (Chapters 8-11) |
| Act IV | Viewing of Seven Pageants (Chapters 12-15) |
| Act V | Pouring Out of Seven Bowls (Chapter 16) |
| Act VI | Unfolding of Seven Plagues (Chapter 17—20:11) |
| Act VII | Fulfillment of God's Sevenfold Plan (Chapters 20:11—21) |
| Epilogue | (Chapter 22) |

"We are living in a time of endurance testing"—this is the theme of the drama. The action moves back and forth between the church and the world. The tribulations and persecutions the church is suffering, and the responses made by the suffering faithful, alternate with the natural catastrophes and wars that convulse the whole earth as scenes within the acts of the drama. There comes a time of judgment:

Revelation
11:18
*"The nations were angry with you, but now it is your turn to be angry with them. It is time to judge the dead, and reward your servants–prophets and people alike, all who fear your Name, both great and small–and to destroy those who have caused destruction upon the earth."*

But God will not force men against their will to participate in the new age. Some will remain in separation:

Revelation
16:10b, 11

*His subjects gnawed their tongues in anguish, and cursed the God of heaven for their pains and sores, but they refused to repent of all their evil deeds.*

For some, the response to the testing is only a curse. For others, whose response is penitence and endurance, what awaits them is beyond human description: a new heaven and a new earth. John tries to describe it anyway. It will be like a new city:

Revelation
21:2a

*I, John, saw the Holy City, the new Jerusalem, coming down from God out of heaven.*

It will be a new and intimate life with God:

Revelation
21:3

*The home of God is now among men, and he will live with them and they will be his people; yes, God himself will be among them.*

It will be an unending comfort to replace the present suffering:

Revelation
21:4

*He will wipe away all tears from their eyes, and there shall be no more death, nor sorrow, nor crying, nor pain. All of that has gone forever.*

In our time the future has been pictured in nearly every imaginable (and some unimaginable) way:

☞  There is the possibility of nuclear holocaust. A few powerful men have the ability, at the press of buttons, to eliminate human life from the earth.

☞  If we survive the nuclear threat, some believe the human race will continue to evolve into a race of supermen and move out over the coming eons to conquer our solar system, our galaxy, the universe.

☞  Others say history is destined to see the overthrow of the rich and the rise of the poor to form a classless society where all attempts of individuals to gain control over one another will wither away.

☞  Some believe human life is a mere accident, unique and alone in the universe. Others think the combination of forces that produced the earth repeated itself thousands of times among the billions of stars and planets.

☞ Many are convinced that belief in God, immortality, and religion are things of the past, at best mere projections of prescientific man's wishes and fears.

☞ Perhaps even more chilling is the belief that there are spiritual forces in the universe we can call "god," but they are malevolent, or at least unconcerned with man. Whatever forces for good there may be are simply too weak to save man from destruction.

☞ There is a school of philosophy that says God and man are both developing; as in nature so with God and man, there is no purpose and much waste, and it is not certain where it will all end.

The first thing to point out in the biblical view of the future is that none of the modern pictures are too horrible or too magnificent to fit in.

The biblical picture of sin and evil, as you have seen, is not merely a list of mistakes human beings make, but deadly, demonic forces of cosmic proportions. People who think there is a divine guarantee against a nuclear holocaust, for example, should be sobered by what happened to the nations like Israel and Judah, blinded by their own self-righteousness, who thought God would never allow their destruction and captivity. (Or consider the deaths by violent means of all other civilizations that have ever lived.)

On the other hand, the biblical view of God's eventual victory is not limited to a mere self-improvement course for a small part of mankind, but is a vision of ultimate redemption on a scale so vast and beautiful that human language breaks under the strain to describe it. That is why it is often difficult to make the biblical descriptions of Heaven and Hell seem real: the metaphors of pearly gates and lakes of fire are trying to express the inexpressible.

The starting point of the biblical view of the future—your future—stretches beyond all the modern pictures; it begins where space becomes infinity, where time becomes eternity, where mortal becomes immortal.

## Getting the Story in Mind

Mark the following statements *True* or *False*.

_____ 1. *The Bible is more concerned about the past than the present or future.*

_____ 2. It is just as well to avoid the parts of the Bible written in symbolic language.

_____ 3. The Book of Revelation is a mysterious book whose meaning only a few learned men can understand.

_____ 4. To think of the Book of Revelation as a play or drama is one way to make it more understandable.

_____ 5. A suffering church and a war-weary world are the settings of the book.

_____ 6. According to the Book of Revelation, a new Heaven and a new earth await believers who endure hardship without putting the blame on God.

_____ 7. Eventually God will step in and force every man to enter his Kingdom.

## Getting the Meaning in Hand

*God In Your Future.* With literally scores of vivid symbols, the Book of Revelation describes eternal life with God and contrasts it to eternal separation from God. Below are twelve pairs of symbols. On the left are symbols of life with God; on the right are symbols of separation. Match the pairs of opposite symbols.

_____ 1. a new city

_____ 2. wedding banquet

_____ 3. "river of the water of life"

_____ 4. a bride clothed in pure linen

_____ 5. paradise

_____ 6. joyous welcome into the city

_____ 7. praising God

_____ 8. "rest from their labors"

_____ 9. great, high mountain

_____ 10. every tear wiped away

_____ 11. a kingdom with the glory of God as its light

_____ 12. God comes down to dwell with men

a. "no rest day or night"

b. bottomless pit

c. city in ruins

d. birds eating carcasses

e. weeping and mourning

f. torment

g. "lake of fire"

h. banned from the city

i. a prostitute dressed in purple and scarlet

j. devil thrown down to earth

k. cursing God

l. a kingdom in darkness

## Side Trip

Modern writers, no less than the biblical ones, have tried to describe their own visions of the future, with its terrors and its rewards. Here is a list of some of the more popular ones; all of which are available in paperback:

Aldous Huxley, *Brave New World*
George Orwell, *1984*
David Riesman, *The Lonely Crowd*
John Kenneth Galbraith, *The Affluent Society*
Kenneth Boulding, *The Meaning of the 20th Century*
Michael Harrington, *The Other America*
Charles Reich, *The Greening of America*
Alvin Toffler, *Future Shock*

In reading or rereading one or more of these works, compare their visions of the future with that of the Bible. At which points do you think the biblical and the modern views are similar, and at which points different?

## 43 The Great Opponent Becomes the Great Believer

*GETTING THE STORY IN MIND*
1   b *(Acts 22:3)*
2   b *(Acts 22:4)*
3   b *(Acts 22:5, 6)*
4   b *(Acts 22:7)*
5   c *(Acts 22:8)*
6   c *(Acts 22:11)*
7   a *(Acts 22:12)*
8   a *(Acts 22:14-16)*

*GETTING THE MEANING IN HAND*
1, 2, 4, 7 *(Acts 22:3, 4; Acts 26:12-20)*

## 44 The Problem of the Hyphenated Christian

*GETTING THE STORY IN MIND*
1   True *(Romans 1:1)*
2   True *(Romans 1:16, 17)*
3   True *(Acts 26:5)*
4   False *(Romans 1:20)*
5   True *(Romans 1:24, 25)*
6   False *(Romans 7:9, 10)*
7   True *(Romans 8:1-4)*

*GETTING THE MEANING IN HAND*
1   Nature *(Romans 1:24, 25)*
2   Nature *(Romans 1:28)*
3   Law *(Romans 3:20)*
4   Law *(Romans 2:16)*
5   Spirit *(Romans 15:13)*
6   Spirit *(Romans 7:25; 12:1)*
7   Nature *(Romans 1:21)*

## 45 Disturber of the Peace, Or Messenger of Peace?

*GETTING THE STORY IN MIND*
1   demonic *(Acts 16:16)*
2   Supreme *(Acts 16:17)*
3   profits *(Acts 16:19)*
4   illegal *(Acts 16:21)*
5   imprisoned *(Acts 16:23)*
6   unfastened *(Acts 16:25)*
7   himself *(Acts 16:27)*
8   believe *(Acts 16:31)*
9   baptized *(Acts 16:33)*
10  Roman *(Acts 16:37)*

*GETTING THE MEANING IN HAND*
1  b *(Acts 16:28, 32)*
2  d *(Acts 16:25)*
3  a *(Acts 16:37)*
4  e *(Acts 16:19)*
5  c *(Acts 16:22, 23, 34)*

## 46  Letters from Prison

*GETTING THE STORY IN MIND*
1  c *(Colossians 1:11)*
2  a *(Colossians 2:1, 2)*
3  d *(Colossians 1:16)*
4  c *(Colossians 1:15-19)*
5  b *(Colossians 2:20-23)*
6  a *(Philemon 16)*
7  d *(Philemon 8-10)*

*GETTING THE MEANING IN HAND*
The "right" answers to these questions are the ones that help you take freedom and bondage a little more seriously, that help you appreciate the freedom you have a little more, and show more compassion toward those still in one of the many kinds of imprisonments the world has to offer.

## 47  Jesus Christ, Incorporated

*GETTING THE STORY IN MIND*
1  b *(1 Corinthians 10:17)*
2  b *(1 Corinthians 6:15)*
3  a *(1 Corinthians 5:1, 2)*
4  c *(1 Corinthians 6:19)*
5  c *(1 Corinthians 11:17, 18)*
6  d *(1 Corinthians 12:12, 13)*
7  c *(1 Corinthians 12:4-11)*
8  b *(1 Corinthians 13)*

*GETTING THE MEANING IN HAND*
1  b *(1 Corinthians 9:27)*
2  a *(1 Corinthians 5:6, 7)*
3  f *(1 Corinthians 12:3)*
4  g *(1 Corinthians 1:10)*
5  c *(1 Corinthians 8:7)*
6  d *(1 Corinthians 5:12, 13)*
7  e *(1 Corinthians 10:16)*

## 48  Enduring to the End

*GETTING THE STORY IN MIND*
1  False *(Revelation 1:1)*
2  False *(Revelation 1:3)*
3  False *(Revelation 2:7)*
4  True *(Compare synopsis [p. 258] with book of Revelation)*
5  True *(Revelation 6:4, 9, 10)*
6  True *(Revelation 14:12, 13)*
7  False *(Revelation 16:10, 11)*

*GETTING THE MEANING IN HAND*

1    c *(Revelation 21:1, 2; 18:19-21)*
2    d *(19:7-9; 19:17, 18)*
3    g *(22:1; 20:10, 14)*
4    i *(21:9; 17:5)*
5    f *(2:7; 14:10)*
6    h *(22:14, 15)*
7    k *(15:3; 16:9-11)*
8    a *(14:13; 14:11)*
9    b *(21:10; 20:1-3)*
10   e *(21:4; 18:9-11)*
11   l *(21:23; 16:10)*
12   j *(21:2, 3; 12:12)*

## FINISHING THE COURSE

Let your progress in this final part of the journey be measured by standards set by earlier followers of God:

*2 Timothy*   below 40   *I have fought long and hard for my Lord. I have kept true to him. Now*
*4:7*                    *the time has come for me to stop fighting and rest.*

*Philippians*   40-49   *Forgetting the past and looking forward to what lies ahead, I*
*3:13*                  *strain to reach the end of the race and receive the prize*
                        *for which God is calling us up to heaven because of what Christ*
                        *Jesus did for us.*

*Philippians*   50-59   *I have learned how to get along happily whether I have much*
*4:11*                  *or little.*

*James*   60-69   *The wisdom that comes from heaven is first of all pure and*
*3:17*            *full of quiet gentleness. Then it is peace-loving and courteous. It*
                  *allows discussion and is willing to yield to others; it is full of*
                  *mercy and good deeds.*

*Hebrews*   70-82   *Let us stop going over the same old ground again and again....*
*6:1-5*             *Let us go on instead to other things...if you have once*
                    *understood the Good News and tasted for yourself the good*
                    *things of heaven and shared in the Holy Spirit, and know how good the*
                    *Word of God is, and felt the mighty powers of the world to come....*

# Epilogue /
## *Where Do We Go from Here?*

We began our biblical journey near the dawn of creation in the
perfect loveliness of the Garden of Eden, where life was free
and goodness suffused all things. Man and woman were
placed in the garden, but they were not forced to stay there,
nor to maintain the innocence in which they had been created.
They were faced with a moral choice. They could choose pride
and rebellion against their loving Creator as well as love for
him. When they made the wrong choice, they began the
moral and physical pollution that still prevents our planet
from being an ideal place to live.

We have followed a drama played out over a span of
centuries in a variety of places in the ancient world. The
main actor was God himself as he sought to save mankind
from slavery—slavery either to other men or to their own
wrong choices—and to call them into a relationship with
himself which would bring them to their greatest stature as
men, and harmonize their relationships among
themselves.

God started with one man who trusted him. Out of
Abraham he created a people. Through his servant Moses
God led his people out of Egypt and bound them to himself
with a covenant. The Law given to Moses showed the kind
of behavior expected of people chosen to be God's special
people. For centuries God worked with this people, ever
with the purpose of eventually reaching all men who would
trust him. God gave his people a good king, David, who
served as a model of kingship for all who followed after
him, for even though he fell into the worst kind of sin, he
came back to God with a heart of true repentance. When
God's people drifted away from him, God sent them
prophets to call them back, to threaten punishment, and
promise redemption. Persecuted in their own times,
prophets like Jeremiah lived on in the memory of the
faithful few who heeded their message and who preserved
their writings through the bitter days of overthrow, exile,
then struggle to maintain freedom in their land once they
returned to it.

In the years between the testaments the people of God
never returned again to the wholesale idol-worship which
corrupted their land in the days of the kings. Their faith was
brightened by the fires of expectation, the belief that any
moment God would fulfill his promise to send a deliverer,
specially anointed to save his people. Some expected a
king to drive out the foreign overlords, some a priest to
purify the faith of God's people, and some a prophet like
Moses to bring God's Word again in a fresh way. In other
ways, though, the intertestamental religion became
hardened. Many people were trusting in their own
obedience to the Law for their salvation, rather than
trusting God himself.

In the fullness of time God did send his own Son, to be a
new kind of king, priest, and prophet, yet hardly anyone
recognized him when he came. Born in an obscure barn
and growing up in the family of a poor manual laborer, he
began to worry the established religious leaders when
people started calling him "Messiah." They plotted to get him
executed by the Roman authorities. Yet this shameful and
agonizing death was the very way in which God chose to
save all men from the shame and agony of their own sins. In

this crucifixion God reconciled all men who would come to him in faith for Jesus' sake, not on the basis of their own merit. And on the third day after Jesus' death, his handful of loyal disciples began to say that they had seen him alive again. God had raised him, and in so doing had given all men the hope of resurrection.

The death and resurrection of Jesus Christ became the good news that spread throughout Jerusalem, Palestine, and the whole Roman Empire, first by Peter and then by other apostles, the most influential of whom was Paul. Small groups of disciples of Jesus sprang up in all the great population centers of the empire, so that the numbers of his followers after his death far exceeded those during his lifetime, for they believed that he was no longer dead, but living and transforming their lives through the spirit he sent them. Not only was Jesus reconciling them to God, but he was reconciling them to each other, harmonizing the differences among Christians of widely varying backgrounds, into one body of Christ, the church.

Many early Christians expected Jesus to come back any moment to complete the transformation of the whole world that he had begun in themselves. As the years and decades passed and the first century after Christ's birth came to a close, the church was beset with persecutions, heresies, organizational problems, and just plain boredom. The writings of Paul are the earliest of the New Testament; the others are generally later and we see the problems of the longer wait coming up. Sceptics began to ask:

2 Peter 3:4 *"So Jesus promised to come back, did he? Then where is he? He'll never come! Why, as far back as anyone can remember everything has remained exactly as it was since the first day of creation."*

For nineteen centuries sceptics have asked that question, and men of faith have replied:

2 Peter 3:9 *"He isn't really being slow about his promised return, even though it sometimes seems that way. But he is waiting, for the good reason that he is not willing that any should perish, and he is giving more time for sinners to repent."*

Even though God is patient, still for men it is not easy to wait.

But waiting is not our main job. God is still alive and active, and his followers must keep going, moving toward a vision that is a combination of a garden of paradise and a new sparkling great city, a vision that fulfills, even surpasses the promises to the patriarchs, the ideal of justice envisioned by the lawgivers, the glorious empires of the kings, the apocalyptic times foreseen by the prophets and apostles.

They followed God. And if we would do so, where do we go from here? To a new heaven and a new earth, no less:

Revelation
21:3, 4

*"I heard a loud shout from the throne saying, "Look, the home of God is now among men, and he will live with them and they will be his people; yes, God himself will be among them. He will wipe away all tears from their eyes, and there shall be no more death, nor sorrow, nor crying, nor pain. All of that has gone forever."*